FRACTALS
A Tool Kit of Dynamics Activities

JONATHAN CHOATE
ROBERT L. DEVANEY
ALICE FOSTER

Key Curriculum Press
Innovators in Mathematics Education

Editor	Masha Albrecht
Editorial Assistants	James A. Browne and Carrye De Mers
Production Editor	Jason Luz
Copyeditor	Joseph Siegel
Interior Designer	Kirk Mills
Layout	Ann Rothenbuhler
Technical Illustration	Ben Turner Graphics
Cover Designer	Kirk Mills
Production and Manufacturing Manager	Diana Jean Parks
Prepress	TSI Graphics
Publisher	Steven Rasmussen
Editorial Director	John Bergez
Executive Editor	Casey FitzSimons

This material is based upon work supported by the National Science Foundation under award number ESI-9255724. Any opinions, findings, and conclusions or recommendations expressed in this publication are those of the authors and do not necessarily reflect the views of the National Science Foundation.

Key Curriculum Press
1150 65th Street
Emeryville, CA 94608
510-595-7000
editorial@keypress.com
http://www.keypress.com

Printed in the United States of America   10 9 8 7 6 5 4 3   04 03 02 01   ISBN 1-55953-355-2

Contents

Curriculum Correlation Key

◔ Small portion of lesson is relevant to indicated stage of curriculum.

◑ About half of lesson is relevant.

● Entire lesson is relevant.

◉ Lesson is particularly relevant and could replace a traditional lesson.

MS   Middle School

A1   Algebra

G   Geometry

A2   Algebra 2

P/C   Precalculus or Calculus

Letter from the Authors

Dear Educator,

Welcome to *Fractals: A Tool Kit of Dynamics Activities*—a unique teaching experience! From the first day that any of us introduced the exciting contemporary topics of iteration, fractals, chaos, and the Julia and Mandelbrot sets into secondary school classrooms, we have been committed to helping others spark interest in their students by exposing them to the beauty and mystery of these rich mathematical topics. In assembling this book, we have attempted to provide you with a blend of explanations, investigations, and teacher information to facilitate your journey into incorporating fractal geometry in your classroom.

Curriculum Links

Although this book can be used as a stand-alone supplementary unit in many mathematics courses, its real strength lies in integrating it within the existing middle school and secondary mathematics curriculum by treating its contents as a contemporary strand of mathematics. Most of us do not have room in an already crowded curriculum to devote an extra week or two to supplementary units but are still searching for materials to enhance existing lessons and topics by incorporating contemporary approaches. Not only do students and teachers find the study of fractals to be intriguing, they also find a strong alignment with topics already present in contemporary mathematics curriculum. For example, Lessons 1 through 6 incorporate many concepts from geometry, such as angles, triangles, congruence, similarity, and transformations. Lessons 9 and 10 deal with logarithms, and Lessons 11 and 12 are developed using geometric series—topics that are part of most second-year algebra programs. By integrating lessons—or even portions of lessons—from these units into your existing curriculum you can introduce students to an exciting and intriguing area of mathematics while building and reinforcing their mathematical thinking on traditional topics.

The Contents pages contain icons that help you identify how specific lessons correlate with different points in the traditional curriculum.

Lesson Contents

At the beginning of each lesson you will find a set of **Teacher Notes**. These notes begin with a short *Overview* of the lesson, which briefly describes the main focus of the lesson. Next, we discuss the *Mathematical Prerequisites* and

Mathematical Connections for this lesson. It is important to note that even though a mathematical topic is listed as a prerequisite, it may in fact be a corequisite, meaning that it can be taught along with the lesson if students have not been exposed to it beforehand.

Technology options are also described to help you make best use of the technology available to you. In some situations, due to the nature of the mathematics, the suggested technology is essential in order to take full advantage of the topic. In particular, Lessons 5 (Random Iteration: The Chaos Game), 6 (Other Chaos Games), and 7 (Rotations and the Chaos Game) will be greatly enhanced if you can access the Java applets at our Web site. The address of this site is **http://math.bu.edu/DYSYS**. Any of the first eight lessons can benefit from the availability of The Geometer's Sketchpad® or any ordinary computer drawing program.

The *Suggested Lesson Plan* section describes the amount of time needed, possible organizational and presentation strategies, and suggested homework assignments. Keep in mind these are only suggestions; your own teaching situation may dictate a different structure or allocation of time. Finally, an assortment of *Lesson Notes* contain suggestions, ideas, and possible extensions.

Some lessons contain **Transparency Masters** designed to be helpful for classroom discussion. These contain copies of diagrams and explanations, and provide you with visuals to aid in student understanding.

The **Explanation** pages introduce the mathematical content of the lesson and are intended for you or your students to read. You may want to photocopy the pages for your students, or you may prefer to summarize the concepts using transparencies. You may also prefer to let your students discover the ideas themselves.

The **Investigations** that follow are in blackline-master format, allowing students to record their answers directly on a photocopy of each page. These are ideal for students to work through cooperatively.

The **Further Exploration** problems extend the ideas from the section. You can photocopy these pages and hand them to students, but they will need to show their work on separate sheets of paper.

Finally, the back of the book contains a thorough and detailed answer to every problem.

Acknowledgments

As with any project that evolves over time, we have many people to thank for their encouragement and assistance. This book grew out of a five-year project sponsored by the National Science Foundation. We are particularly indebted to James Sandefur and Spud Bradley of NSF for their support during this period. Many teachers participated in the four-year series of summer workshops that helped to define these materials. We are most appreciative of the efforts of the lead teachers in these efforts: Beverly Mawn, Jamil Siddiqui, Rob Quaden, Liz Perry, John Bookston, Al Coons, Kathy Leggat, Megan Staples, Jim Carpenter, and Gerald Nimetz. Eileen Lee contributed enormously to the project in the early stages by refining and elaborating on our original notes, and Megan Staples helped put everything together with some excellent hints and tips for teachers and students in the solutions to the exercises. Numerous people contributed to the technology portion of this project, including Clara Bodelon, Rodin Enchev, Noah Goodmann, Kevin Lee, Alex Kasman, Adrian Vajiac, and Johanna Voolich. Finally, it is a pleasure to thank all of the folks at Key Curriculum Press, especially Steve Rasmussen, Jason Luz, and Masha Albrecht, for their enthusiasm and helpfulness in bringing this project to a successful conclusion.

We hope you will find the teacher materials helpful and the mathematical content exciting and challenging. Welcome to our chaotic world!

Jonathan Choate
Robert L. Devaney
Alice Foster

INTRODUCTION: WHY FRACTALS?

In this book we will describe some of the wonderful new ideas in the area of mathematics known as fractal geometry. As you will see, fractals are incredibly complicated and often quite beautiful geometric shapes that can be generated by simple rules.

The images we call fractals have been known in mathematics for well over a century. Objects such as the Cantor set, the Sierpiński triangle, and the Koch curve—all shapes that we will encounter many times in the next few pages— have appeared often in the mathematical literature over the past hundred years. However, these objects were once regarded as almost pathological shapes mainly of interest in mathematical research.

All of this has changed in the last 20 years. Two events occurred in that period that brought fractal geometry into the mainstream of contemporary science and mathematics. The first was the observation by the mathematician Benoit Mandelbrot that fractals are not just mathematical curiosities, but rather the geometry of nature. He observed that many objects in the natural world were fractal in appearance. Ferns, clouds, trees, coastlines, and many other "irregular shapes" could best be understood using fractal geometry rather than Euclidean geometry. Indeed, while the straight lines, triangles, and circles of Euclidean geometry are important for humans to build bridges, houses, roads, and the like, nature seems to construct its objects differently. Natural objects are often more complicated and have a richer geometry. As we will see, they can often be modeled with fractals.

The second event that brought fractal geometry into the limelight was the availability of computers. Before people had access to computers and computer graphics, fractals could only be envisioned in the mind. They were often too complicated for a human to draw and too difficult to explain to others. The computer changed this dramatically. When mathematicians could see the structure of the objects they were working with, they realized that the objects were much more interesting and beautiful than they had previously thought. Moreover, the computer allowed mathematicians to discover many more exciting examples of fractals that no one had imagined before. This includes the gorgeous images known as the Mandelbrot and Julia sets that we will investigate in a later booklet.

People now use and study fractals in many more areas than just mathematics. Fractals arise in medicine: Cancerous tumors, human lungs, and vascular systems are all examples of fractals. Art historians use fractals to date early Chinese paintings. Seismologists use fractals to study the fissures caused by earthquakes. Computer programmers use fractal techniques to encode large sets of data efficiently. Fractals even occur in Broadway plays (such as Tom Stoppard's *Arcadia*) and in films (such as *Jurassic Park*), where they are used to create extraterrestrial planet-scapes and other special effects.

One goal of this book is to show you many different ways of building fractal images. We will also describe how fractal geometry relates to many other areas of mathematics that you are studying, including ordinary plane geometry and algebra. Of course, since fractals are so intimately related to computation, we hope that you have some access to a computer and calculator as you read through these pages. There are many different fractal programs currently available, and you may want to use at least one in conjunction with this book. We have constructed a special Web site that contains different programs that you can use to investigate various aspects of fractal geometry. Please visit us at **http://math.bu.edu/DYSYS**.

We hope you have fun learning this material. We also hope that it excites you as much as it has us.

Geometric Iteration

OVERVIEW

This lesson introduces the basic concepts of iteration from a geometric approach. Students practice applying geometric iteration rules to generate a sequence of figures and then predict the "fate" of that sequence. The resulting fractal images include such famous fractals as the Sierpiński triangle and the Cantor middle-thirds set. If students have previously worked with any units from the first book, *Iteration: A Tool Kit of Dynamics Activities,* then much of the terminology will be familiar to them. (In fact, this lesson is identical to Lesson 6 in *Iteration.*) If not, then you may need to spend a little more time making sure students understand the basic concept of iteration and terms such as *seed, orbit, iterate, period* and *cycle* as they are introduced.

MATHEMATICAL PREREQUISITES

Students need to be familiar with basic geometric shapes, degree measure, rotation, "shrinking" or dilation, and midpoints. For certain exercises, students need to be familiar with either the Pythagorean theorem or the properties of a 45°-45°-90° triangle.

MATHEMATICAL CONNECTIONS

Topics from your mathematics curriculum that have connections to this lesson are **similar figures** and **ratios of similarity**, **geometric transformations**, **geometric sequences**, **exponential growth** and **decay**, and an introductory concept of **limits**. Links to more specific concepts and skills are included in the Lesson Notes below and in teacher annotations to the solutions.

TECHNOLOGY

You can use computer graphics programs, or even a simple drawing program, to investigate geometric iteration. Also, a spreadsheet—or table feature on a graphing calculator—might be used to calculate lengths of sides and successive perimeters and areas. Several other investigations are well suited to The Geometer's Sketchpad®.

SUGGESTED LESSON PLAN

CLASS TIME

One to two 50-minute class periods, depending on how much is assigned outside of class.

PREPARATION

Depending on where you are in your curriculum, you might want to review some basic geometric shapes, degree measurements, the Pythagorean theorem, and the 45°-45°-90° triangle, or you may prefer to use this lesson as a means of revisiting those topics as they come up.

LESSON DEVELOPMENT

△ Have students read at least the first two paragraphs of the first Explanation page for homework prior to presenting this lesson. They might also read this at the beginning of class. You might photocopy only this first page and not the rest of the Explanation pages. You can even copy the first two paragraphs as a half page.

△ Ask students to summarize key points—or ask them to define or explain key terms (for example, *seed, iteration rule, orbit, fate of orbit*).

Possible questions:

1. What do we mean by the term *iteration?*

2. What two items are necessary in order to perform a geometric iteration? (*Answer:* a seed and an iteration rule. If your students have previously worked with the book *Iteration* that is in this series, ask them to recall the process of numerical iteration.)

3. Did the reading ever define the word *fractal?*

△ Use transparencies 1A and 1B and the information in the rest of the Explanation pages to investigate several different types of iteration rules as a class. (See the Lesson Notes that follow for discussion ideas.)

Note: You can start demonstrations of the "seed" concept with the stick figure and the "Hi" configuration on Transparency 1A so students can try these at their seats. After discussing the "shrinking" square, you might draw the first iteration of the stick figure on your transparency, then have students continue the orbit on their worksheet so they get the feel for the process. Then have them try the "Hi" configuration and discuss any questions about its "fate" before proceeding to the rotating iteration items on Transparency 1B. Remember, the transparencies were designed so you could cover up portions of them and "reveal" pictures in the orbit when appropriate.

⌂ After discussing the rotation examples, you could have students work on Investigations 1 and 2 in class or for homework as time permits.

HOMEWORK SUGGESTIONS

⌂ If students complete Investigations 1 and 2 in class:

Assign some or all of the remaining Investigations and/or Further Exploration problems for homework. Depending on the level of your class, you might not want to assign a table-making investigation (3, 5, and 6) until after you have worked through one with students in class. Reading through the Lesson Notes or the Answers for these investigations will give you a better feel for which ones are appropriate for your students.

⌂ If you plan to use two 50-minute class periods:

After addressing questions arising from the homework, have students work on either Investigation 3 (if they are familiar with the 45°-45°-90° or the Pythagorean theorem—see Lesson Notes) or Investigation 5 to familiarize them with completing the orbit tables. These types of tables are used in several other lessons and provide students with a good tool for organizing data. Then Investigations 4 and 6 and the Further Exploration problems could be used for homework.

LESSON NOTES

A SHRINKING ITERATION RULE

Students may overlook the fact that only the "linear" dimension is cut in half. Make sure they understand that the "area" is not cut in half. This would be an excellent opportunity to discuss the ratio of the areas of similar figures being the square of the ratio of similarity. (In upper level courses, such as advanced algebra and precalculus, you may want to actually write out the sequences for the orbits of the perimeters and areas and discuss the fact that they are geometric sequences.)

For the stick figure example, make sure that students understand "decreasing by a factor of 2" is the same as "shrinking by $\frac{1}{2}$"; students often have difficulty describing the same operation in these two different ways. To reinforce the concept, you might ask them: What would it mean if we decreased each iteration by a factor of 3? by a factor of 10? (This is actually a good opportunity to stress in middle school the relationship between division and fractions.)

In the "Hi" example, some students may insist that the fate of the orbit is two points, not one. Emphasize that the distance between the two letters is also cut in half each time. If they still have difficulty seeing this, you might have a student face a wall and act out the rule of decreasing his or her distance from the wall by one-half at each iteration. Although the student never actually becomes the wall, the distance between them becomes so negligible that for all practical purposes they have reached the same "point."

A ROTATING ITERATION RULE

In the discussion regarding the circle remaining "fixed" at each iteration, you may want to discuss the importance in mathematics of agreeing upon definitions or parameters for a problem. In this case, we are agreeing that an orbit will be described in terms of what happens to the apparent orientation of the overall shape. One way to reinforce this issue might be to ask students if they can think of another figure whose orbit appears to be fixed under a 90° rotation (e.g., a filled square). Or, you might reverse the question and ask what rotation would be needed for the orbit of an equilateral triangle to be fixed. (Students are apt to answer 60°, rather than the correct 120°; you might need to demonstrate the rotation to help them see this. Part of the discussion should focus on the fact that the triangle could rotate onto its own image exactly three times to complete a 360° rotation; so the orbit is a cycle of period 3, and 360° divided by the 3 periods is 120°. For middle school students, the concepts being developed here link well to future understanding in geometry and trigonometry, and for students already in those courses, the curriculum connections could be pointed out for reinforcement.

INVESTIGATIONS 1 AND 2

To illustrate these in a computer drawing program, draw the initial figure (in the case of Investigation 1, "group" the two lines to form a single figure), make a duplicate of the figure, and shrink it by 50% using the scaling or dilation feature of the drawing program. Then copy that iteration and shrink again. Continue until the "fate" of the orbit becomes obvious.

INVESTIGATION 3

To complete the table students need to be familiar with square roots (including leaving answers in radical form) and either the Pythagorean theorem or the side-length relationships for a 45°-45°-90° triangle. If students are not familiar with these concepts, we suggest you skip this Investigation.

It is *not* advisable to use either a spreadsheet or table feature of a graphing calculator to generate this particular table due to the necessity of keeping $\sqrt{2}$ in radical form in order to be able to express the nth iteration.

In upper level classes (advanced algebra and higher) this is an excellent place to make connections to geometric sequences and limits.

INVESTIGATION 4

You might have students come to the board or overhead to draw the next iteration until someone in the class feels they can describe the fate of the orbit.

Questions you might ask are: How many circles will there be in the fourth iteration? How can you determine the number of circles you will have in any iteration from the number of circles in the previous one? Eventually try to get students to see that the number of circles in the nth iteration equals the number of circles in the previous $(n - 1)$ iteration times 2. The level of mathematical sophistication (in terms of notation) that you arrive at depends on the mathematical level of your students. Still, for this investigation even middle school students should be able to "describe" that the number of circles doubles each time and to begin assessing whether the "length" of the object doubles. Students may see that the orbit tends toward a segment, but they may miss the fact that it is a particular segment, namely, the diameter of the original circle.

The stick figure may be even harder for students to follow through its orbit; in this instance, using a drawing program and the size reduction feature may be really helpful. *Note:* For a little exercise in critical thinking, you might ask students to consider what assumption was made about the stick figure drawing that resulted in the length of the line segment being equal to the distance between the legs of the original figure. (*Answer:* The distance between the legs was assumed to be the widest part of the original figure. How would the fate of the orbit change if the widest part of the figure was the arm span?)

INVESTIGATION 5

The Geometer's Sketchpad or a drawing program can be used to generate more iterations of this fractal. For students who need a more tactile approach, have them actually draw an equilateral triangle, locate the midpoints carefully by measuring, and connect the midpoints to form the inner triangle. Have them repeat the process for several iterations, being careful to *shade* and *unshade* the appropriate triangles at each step. Hexagonal dot paper might be helpful.

In order to prepare students for completing the table, you might want to pose the questions: How many triangles will there be after the fifth iteration (81 times 3, or 3 to the fifth power)? How many after the fifteenth iteration (3 to the fifteenth power)?

For upper level students, have them add two more rows to the table: one tracing the orbit of the perimeter and one tracing the orbit of the area. (How does the area of each iteration compare to the area of the previous iteration, and how does the perimeter of each iteration compare to the perimeter of the previous iteration?) Then have them plot these orbits, look at the graphs as exponential growth and decay graphs, and discuss the perplexing situation of a "geometric figure" with increasing perimeter and decreasing area.

Another interesting discussion for upper level classes focuses on the function $y = A(\frac{3}{4})^n$ as a way to express the area of any iteration, n, given A as the original area. If students plot this exponential decay graph, an interesting question to pose is: What, if anything, does the graph mean for $n = 2.5$? Obviously nothing, since you can't have iteration number two and one-half! This allows you to discuss the difference between discrete and continuous functions and graphs and to point out that iteration is a discrete, rather than continuous, process.

INVESTIGATION 6

Here is a marvelous opportunity to have students do some serious thinking about fractions! In addition to determining the lengths of the remaining segments at each iteration, have students determine the locations of the endpoints on a ruler going from 0 to 1. This approach to the Cantor middle-thirds set is actually discussed in the answers to Investigation 7 in Lesson 3: Self-Similarity, but you might want to get students to start thinking about it here.

FRACTALS: A TOOL KIT OF DYNAMICS ACTIVITIES
©1999 KEY CURRICULUM PRESS

Shrinking Iteration Rules

Seed: A square with sides of length 1

Rule: Shrink the figure so that each side is half as long.

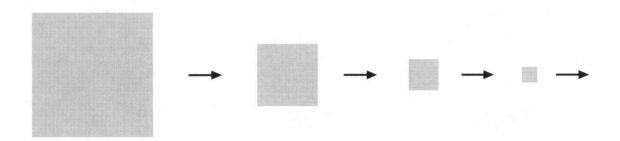

Try the same rule with this seed:

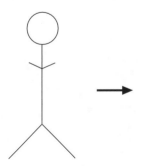

Try another seed:

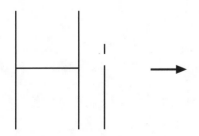

Rotating Iteration Rules

Seed: "Ellipse" with a face

Rule: Rotate the seed 90° clockwise

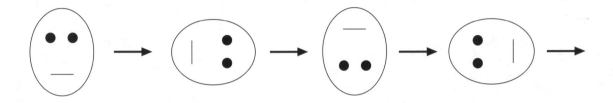

Description of orbit: Cycle of period 4

Try the same rule with this seed:

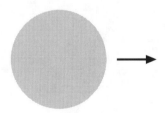

Description of orbit:

FRACTALS: A TOOL KIT OF DYNAMICS ACTIVITIES
©1999 KEY CURRICULUM PRESS

NAME(S):

We begin the study of fractals by introducing one of the main processes by which fractals are generated, namely, iteration. **Iteration** means to repeat a process over and over again. There are many types of iterative processes in mathematics. Some involve algebraic equations or mathematical functions. Others involve computer algorithms. In this lesson, most of our iterations will involve a geometric rule or construction. We begin with some geometric shape or figure called the **seed**. Then we perform a geometric operation on this seed. This geometric operation is called the **iteration rule**. The rule might involve rotating or squeezing or cutting apart the shape. After we perform this operation we obtain a new figure. Then we iterate; this means we perform the same operation on the new figure to produce the next figure. We then repeat this process, continually applying the iteration rule to produce a sequence of figures.

This sequence of shapes has a name. It is called the **orbit** of the geometric iteration. Our main question is: What is the shape that ultimately results when we apply this geometric iteration over and over? This is the same as asking: What is the "fate" of the orbit? As we will see, simple geometric iterations can lead to the very complicated results known as fractals.

A SHRINKING ITERATION RULE

Let's begin with a simple example of a geometric iteration. The seed is a square whose sides each have length 1. The iteration rule is: "Shrink the square so that each side is half as long." We can picture the orbit as a sequence of squares. Each succeeding square has linear dimensions equal to half that of the preceding square. The orbit is:

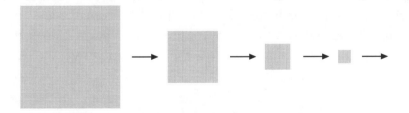

As we iterate this rule, the squares in the orbit shrink so that their sides have smaller and smaller length. That is, the squares are tending toward a single point. Therefore, the limiting shape or the fate of this orbit is a single point.

Here is another example. This time we start with another seed, a stick figure, but use the same iteration rule:

Again, the length and width of the figure decrease at each iteration by a factor of 2, and the stick figures gradually shrink and approach a single point.

Here is another example of the same iteration rule but with a different seed. The seed is the word "Hi," and the iteration rule is the same as the previous two—namely, shrink everything by a factor of 2. So the first few images in the orbit are:

At each stage both the "H" and the "i" shrink in size and move closer together. As we continue to iterate, the letter shapes "H" and "i" get smaller and smaller and closer and closer, so the end result of this iteration is again a single point. Note that the fate is not two points, because the distance between the "H" and the "i" is continually halved as we iterate.

A ROTATING ITERATION RULE

Here is a different iteration rule: Start with some figure in the plane and rotate it 90° clockwise. In the following, the orbit repeats itself after every fourth iteration, so we say that this orbit is a **cycle of period 4**:

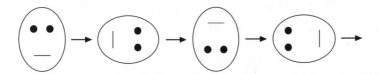

But what happens if we start with a filled circle as the seed and keep the preceding iteration rule? Then the orbit of this seed is:

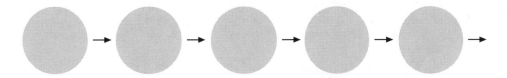

We say this orbit is **fixed**, because the picture never changes; it always remains the same. (Actually, since we are rotating this circle at each stage, the points inside the circle are rotating; the points themselves aren't really fixed. What is important here is that the picture at each stage remains the same—it always looks like the same circle. So we think of this picture that remains unchanged at each iteration as an orbit that remains fixed.)

If we start with a rectangle and apply this iteration rule, then the orbit becomes a **cycle of period 2**:

As before, any point in this picture (except the center of the rectangle) returns to itself after four iterations, but the picture itself is the same after two iterations.

Name(s):

TECHNOLOGY TIP

You can perform the first two investigations more efficiently in almost any computer drawing program.

1 ▷ A SHRINKING ITERATION RULE

a. Sketch the next three pictures in the orbit using the iteration rule: "Shrink the previous figure so that each side is one-half as long and one-half as wide."

b. Now make up your own seed, but use the same rule as in (a).

⟶

c. What happens to each of the orbits described in (a) and (b)?

_____

d. Does the orbit described in (a) approach one point or two points? Why?

_____

2 ▷ A ROTATING ITERATION RULE

Sketch the first four pictures in the orbit using the suggested seeds. Use this iteration rule: "Rotate the figure 90° clockwise."

After you have drawn the first four pictures, describe the fate of each orbit.

a. Your seed is a square.

_____

b. Your seed is an ellipse.

_____

c. Your seed is a picture of a banana.

_____

3 ▷ A MIDPOINT ITERATION RULE

For this investigation your seed is a square and its interior. Use the following iteration rule: "First sketch the boundary of the previous square. Then find the midpoint of each side. Connect adjacent midpoints with a straight line segment to form a new square. Then remove the old square and shade the interior of the new square."

a. Sketch the first few pictures in the orbit, then describe the orbit in words.

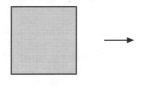

_____

b. Assume the length of a side of the original square is 1. Complete the table below by calculating the side length and area of each square. Use the last column to generalize your findings by writing directions for finding the area and side length for any square in the orbit.

	Original square (the seed)	First iteration	Second iteration	Third iteration	nth iteration
Side length	1 unit				
Area					

TECHNOLOGY TIP

You can make a larger version of a table like this on a spreadsheet.

4 ▷ A REPLACEMENT ITERATION RULE

Geometric iterations can become more complicated. For example, consider what happens with this iteration rule: "Replace a circle by two smaller copies of itself whose diameters are each one-half of the original. Line up the smaller circles side by side."

a. Draw the next two images in this orbit. What is happening to this orbit as we continue to iterate? What is the fate of the orbit? Are these pictures tending toward a particular picture?

_____

_____

b. What is the fate of this orbit if the seed is a square? A rectangle? A stick figure?

_____

_____

_____

NAME(S):

TECHNOLOGY TIP

You can use The Geometer's Sketchpad to build a script that can create either of the next two fractals to higher iterations.

5 ▷ FAMOUS FRACTAL 1

Here is a simple example of a geometric iteration that you will encounter often in future work with iteration and fractals. The seed is the solid triangle. The iteration rule is: "Remove a triangle from the middle of the given triangle so that three congruent triangles remain." The seed and first iteration are shown below.

a. Draw the next figure in this orbit. You will now need to use your rule three times, once on each of the three solid triangles.

b. Draw at least one more figure in this orbit.

c. If we continue this process, after infinitely many steps we will have removed the middles of all triangles. What remains is a very complicated figure: a well-known fractal called the Sierpiński triangle. Use your observations to write a short paragraph describing this fractal.

_____

_____

_____

d. Now complete the table below.

	Original triangle (the seed)	First iteration	Second iteration	Third iteration	nth iteration
Total number of triangles remaining	1	3			
Side length of each triangle	1				

6 ▷ FAMOUS FRACTAL 2

Here is another iteration rule that also produces a fractal image. The seed is a straight line segment, including its endpoints. The iteration rule is: "Remove the middle third of any segment, leaving behind the endpoints."

a. Draw the first few figures in this orbit.

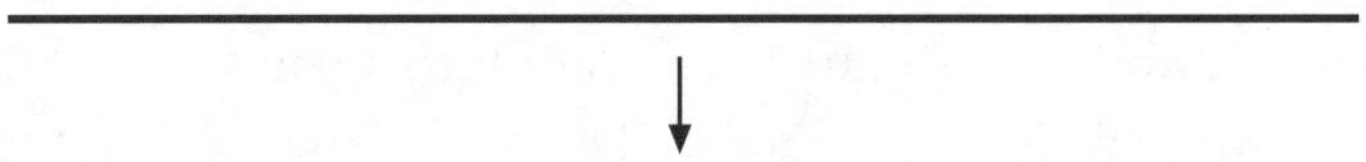

↓

b. If we continue this process, after infinitely many steps we have another well-known fractal: the Cantor middle-thirds set. Use your observations to write a short paragraph describing this fractal.

_____

_____

_____

c. Now complete the table below.

	Original segment (the seed)	First iteration	Second iteration	Third iteration	nth iteration
Total number of segments remaining	1	2			
Length of each segment	1				

d. Are there any points from the original segment that remain in the orbit for *all* iterations? Explain.

_____

_____

FRACTALS: A TOOL KIT OF DYNAMICS ACTIVITIES
©1999 KEY CURRICULUM PRESS

Each of the eight problems below shows an iteration rule and a seed. Pick one or more of these rules. Show all your work carefully on another sheet of paper.

▲ Draw the seed and the next three figures in the orbit.

▲ Describe as much as you can about the orbit. This includes describing the number and the lengths of the shapes at each iteration.

▲ In some cases, the resulting image is a fractal and already has a name. Find out this name if you can. If not, name the fractal yourself.

▲ Try to model the seed and iteration process using technology. Describe the technology you use and include any appropriate printouts, sketches, or programs.

1. The seed is an equilateral triangle. The iteration rule is: "Join the midpoints of each of the sides of the triangle to form a new triangle."

2. The seed is a right triangle. The iteration rule is the same as in problem 1. How does the type of triangle change your results?

3. The seed is a straight line segment. The iteration rule is to remove the middle third of each segment and then replace it with two other segments, each of whose length is one-third the length of the original. That is, the rule converts each straight segment into four segments, arranged as in the picture, and each segment is one-third as long as the original segment.

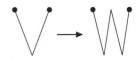

4. a. In this iteration, the seed is a circle. The iteration rule is to place a circle of the same size just to the right of the previous circle.

   b. In this iteration, the seed is a circle. The iteration rule is to place an exact copy of the previous figure just to the right of the previous figure. (Note that while the second figure in this orbit is the same as in the previous rule, subsequent figures will be different.)

5. In this case the seed is a "V." The iteration rule can be described this way: Think of the two endpoints at the top of the "V" as being tacked down. Then replace the "V" with a "W" whose endpoints are the same. That is, the "V" is replaced with two copies of itself that are squeezed together.

V → W

6. The seed is a circle whose diameter is 1. The iteration rule is: "Replace this circle with two circles, each of whose diameters is one-third of the original diameter and which are located as shown here. Only the two gray circles remain, not the outline of the original circle."

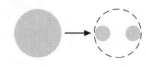

7. The seed is a rectangle. The iteration rule is to cut the rectangle vertically into three equal-sized pieces and remove the middle third, leaving behind the vertical boundaries of the removed piece.

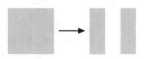

FRACTALS: A TOOL KIT OF DYNAMICS ACTIVITIES
©1999 KEY CURRICULUM PRESS

Fractals Generated by Removals

OVERVIEW

The purpose of this lesson is to introduce students to a number of fractals that are created by following a specific set of rules. Such fractals are referred to as **deterministic** fractals because their fate is determined by successive applications of the rules. All rules in this lesson involve dividing an image into smaller pieces, similar to the original and congruent to each other, and then removing some of those pieces. In creating these various fractal images, students should begin to develop an informal concept of what fractals are (or are not) before any formal properties of fractals are introduced. The investigations offer students additional practice with the concept of geometric iteration and with the importance of following directions carefully.

MATHEMATICAL PREREQUISITES

Students need to be familiar with basic geometric shapes and concepts such as equilateral triangles, right triangles, congruent triangles, interior of a geometric figure, regular polygons, and exponents.

MATHEMATICAL CONNECTIONS

Topics from your mathematics curriculum that have connections to this lesson are **fractions, perimeter, area, symmetry, congruence, similarity,** and **ratios of similarity**. In upper level courses, connections can be made to **exponential growth** and **decay** as well as **continuous** versus **discrete** functions. To make these connections, graph the nth iteration formulas identified in the tables and discuss the "behavior" of the successive iterations. The Lesson Notes below and answers in the back describe links to more specific concepts and skills.

TECHNOLOGY

You can use spreadsheets or the table feature of a graphing calculator to generate successive side lengths, perimeters, and areas of each iteration. This would give students practice in describing a mathematical process and expressing it in terms of a "formula."

SUGGESTED LESSON PLAN

CLASS TIME

Two 50-minute class periods. In the first class, you could introduce the process of generating fractals by removals and have students practice some on their own before doing the homework. In the second class, students could work in cooperative groups on the Further Exploration problems.

PREPARATION

The teacher should read through the Explanation pages and introduce students to the material by using transparencies in an interactive classroom discussion. Although students could be given copies of the Explanation pages to read through on their own, the extremely visual nature of this topic probably lends itself better to a classroom discussion in which students actually draw their own images first rather than reading about them.

LESSON DEVELOPMENT

DAY 1

▲ Use Transparency 2A to introduce the material on generating the Sierpiński triangle by removals.

1. Explain the iteration rule and demonstrate the first removal on the first set of triangles on the transparency.

2. Have students sketch the next two iterations at their seats.

3. Reveal only the "More images in the orbit" section of Transparency 2B and discuss any concerns.

4. Have students try to describe the fate of this orbit, then reveal the Sierpiński triangle on Transparency 2B.

▲ Repeat this process with the "Fractal Plus" and the "Fractal H," using Transparencies 2B and 2C. In each case, make sure students understand the rule; possibly show them the first iteration from your transparencies. You may want students to sketch these orbits on graph paper to save time.

▲ Give students directions for generating the "non-fractal" from the Explanation pages. Have them generate the image, then discuss how it differs from the others. Be sure to tell them this one is not a fractal, and see if they can begin to describe some of the differences between figures that are fractals and those that are not. In this case the segment does not seem to be a fractal because it is too simple a shape. The precise reason a segment is not a fractal (which you do not need to share with students at this stage) is because its fractal dimension and its topological dimension are equal. In fact, both equal 1. Dimension is discussed in Lesson 9: Fractal Dimension.

▲ Assign Investigations 1–4 for homework.

DAY 2

After discussing solutions to the Investigations, have students work on the Further Exploration problems in class in cooperative groups. Problems 5–8 are challenging. You might want to work through one of these as a class if students are having difficulty with them.

LESSON NOTES

SYMMETRY IN THE INTRODUCTORY EXAMPLES

These three sample fractals offer an excellent opportunity for discussing **symmetry.** You might have students identify lines of symmetry for each of these three examples and pose questions such as: Does the Fractal H have as many lines of symmetry as the Fractal Plus?

DIVISIBILITY AS APPLIED TO THE FRACTAL PLUS AND THE FRACTAL H

These two fractals will be much easier for students to generate using graph paper. This raises the interesting problem of how big to make the seed so that it can easily be subdivided for several iterations. Students might start with a 30-by-30 grid and successfully subdivide that into thirds for the next iteration. Then you could ask how they divide the new 10-by-10 grids into thirds. A nice discussion could emerge regarding the fact that the length of the grid must not only be divisible by 3, but the remaining factor must also be divisible by 3. So the largest seed you could fit on the graph paper and still continue subdividing

would be 27 by 27. You might also ask what the next larger size grid would have to be (81 by 81) and what the largest seed would be if you wanted to subdivide into fourths instead of thirds. ·

INVESTIGATIONS 1–4

You might have students think about what is happening to the area and "perimeter" of these figures even though those items are not listed in the tables. In high school level classes you might look at the exponential growth and decay of the number of squares remaining, the lengths of the sides, and the area and the perimeter. To do this, enter the nth iteration formulas into a graphing calculator and plot the "size" or number of items against the number of the iteration. In upper level courses you might also discuss continuous versus discrete functions by asking whether it makes sense to have a point on the graph showing length for the one-and-one-half iteration.

Generating Fractals by "Removals"

Seed: An equilateral triangle and its interior.

Rule: Remove a triangle from the middle of the original triangle so that:

▴ The sides are one-half the length of the original.

▴ Three congruent triangles remain.

Sketch the next figure:

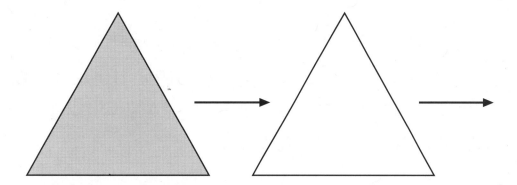

Now sketch the next two images in the orbit.

More images in the orbit:

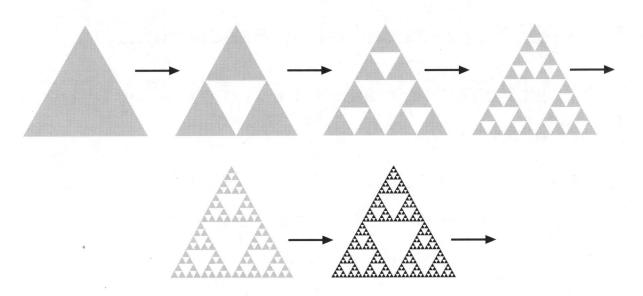

It's the Sierpiński triangle!

Sketch the next figures in the orbit of the Fractal Plus. (*Hint:* Use graph paper and start with a big square. Pick the size carefully!)

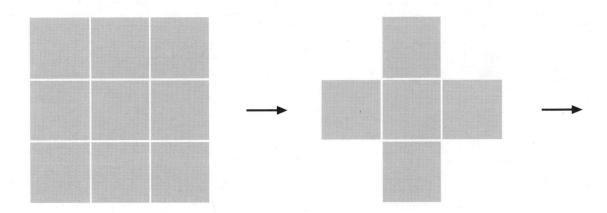

More images in the Fractal Plus orbit:

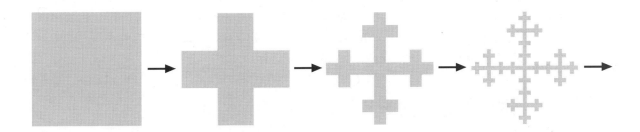

And eventually:

Now try a Fractal H.

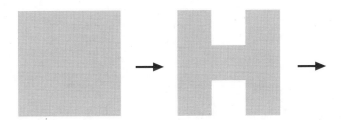

More figures in the Fractal H orbit:

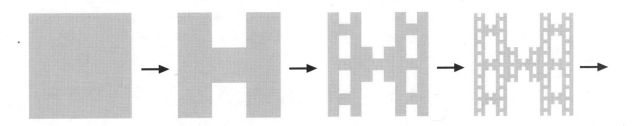

Before describing exactly what a fractal is, let's first look at a number of different examples of fractals. There are several different methods you can use to construct a fractal. In this lesson the methods are **deterministic**. That means that our fractals will be constructed according to specific rules that are set down ahead of time. In another lesson you will investigate random fractals, where the rules are quite different.

THE SIERPIŃSKI TRIANGLE

In one of the standard methods of constructing fractals, the iteration rule involves successive "removals." To construct the shape known as the Sierpiński triangle, we begin with an equilateral triangle as the seed and then use the iteration rule: "Remove from the middle of this triangle a smaller triangle with side lengths one-half those of the original so that three congruent triangles remain." Geometrically, this iteration rule is expressed by the images above.

The orbit is then:

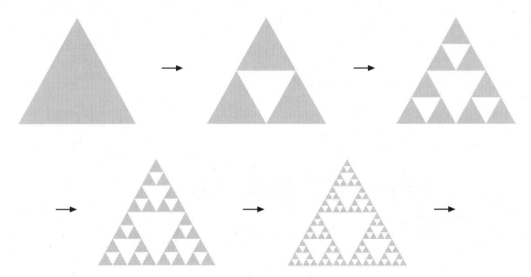

There is one technical, but important, detail. When you remove each triangle, you actually remove only the triangle's interior, not its boundary. The sides and vertices of each removed triangle remain as part of the next figure in the orbit.

When this rule is iterated infinitely often, you reach a limiting shape known as the Sierpiński triangle. This is one of the simplest examples of the geometric objects known as **fractals**.

Let's just look at a few more geometric objects constructed in this manner.

THE FRACTAL PLUS

Here is another geometric iteration that results in a fractal. Start with a square whose side has length 1. The iteration rule is to first divide the square into nine squares whose sides have length $\frac{1}{3}$. Then remove the four corner squares as shown here:

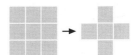

After this first iteration, five squares remain. Each of them has sides of length $\frac{1}{3}$ and area $\frac{1}{9}$. Now we iterate. At the next iteration we find 25 squares, each with sides of length $\frac{1}{9}$ and area $\frac{1}{81}$. At the third iteration we have 125 squares with sides of length $\frac{1}{27}$, and so forth.

If we continue this process forever, the squares get smaller and the eventual image is a "fractal plus sign" like the one at right.

THE FRACTAL H

Here is a similar iteration rule. As done for the Fractal Plus, we begin with a square that has been subdivided into nine smaller squares. This time we remove only two of the smaller squares, leaving behind the shape of an "H." Here are the first three figures in this orbit:

When we apply this rule over and over, a new fractal results:

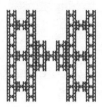

A NON-FRACTAL

Not all processes involving removals lead to fractal
images. For example, consider the following iteration
rule. Start with a square whose sides have length 1.
Then divide the square horizontally into two congruent rectangles. Each will
have length 1 and width $\frac{1}{2}$. Remove the upper rectangle, leaving behind the
bottom rectangle.

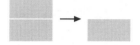

After one more iteration the remaining rectangle has width $\frac{1}{4}$.

If we continue the process indefinitely, the shape approaches a segment whose
length is the same as the side of the original square. Whatever a fractal is, it is
not a segment, so *this* process of removals does *not* generate a fractal.

All of the fractals in this section were generated by removing certain pieces of
"regular" geometric figures. We will encounter other ways of constructing
fractals in other lessons.

1 ▷ THE SIERPIŃSKI CARPET

The Sierpiński carpet is generated by the following iteration rule: Begin with a square whose side has length 1. Then divide the square into nine equal-sized squares whose sides have length ⅓. Remove the middle square, leaving eight smaller squares behind.

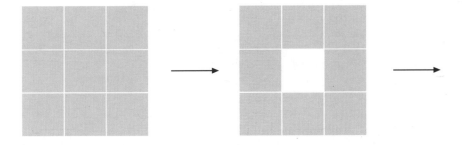

a. Draw the next figure in this orbit.

b. Now complete the table below.

	Original square (the seed)	First iteration	Second iteration	Third iteration	*n*th iteration
Total number of squares remaining	1	8			
Side length of each square	1	$\frac{1}{3}$			

2 ▷ THE FRACTAL X

What happens when we consider the following modification of the preceding iteration rule? Again, start with a square of length 1. Break this square into nine pieces as above, but this time remove four squares as shown here:

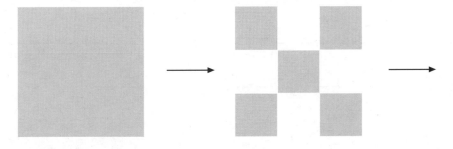

a. Draw the next figure in this orbit.

b. Now complete the table below.

	Original square (the seed)	First iteration	Second iteration	Third iteration	nth iteration
Total number of squares remaining	1				
Side length of each square	1				

c. What do you think the resulting figure will look like?

_____

3 ▷ THE DIAGONAL

Suppose we modify the above iteration rule so that only three squares lying on a diagonal line remain after the removals, as in this picture:

a. Draw the next two figures in this orbit.

b. Now complete the table below.

	Original square (the seed)	First iteration	Second iteration	Third iteration	nth iteration
Total number of squares remaining	1				
Side length of each square	1				

FRACTALS: A TOOL KIT OF DYNAMICS ACTIVITIES
©1999 KEY CURRICULUM PRESS

c. What do you think the resulting figure will look like?

_____

_____

d. Would you call this figure a fractal? Why or why not?

_____

_____

4 ▷ REMOVING A CORNER

Consider the following iteration rule that also involves removals. Start with a square whose sides have length 1. Then divide the square into four squares, each of which have sides of length ½. Finally, remove the upper right square, leaving three squares behind in an "L" shape:

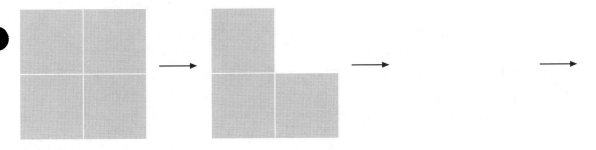

a. First draw the next two figures in this orbit.

b. Now complete the table below.

	Original square (the seed)	First iteration	Second iteration	Third iteration	nth iteration
Total number of squares remaining	1				
Side length of each square	1				

c. What do you think will be the ultimate shape if you continue this process?

_____

For each of the following iteration rules, first draw several subsequent figures in the orbit on a separate sheet of paper. Then describe what you think the final figure will look like.

1. Begin with a square. Divide the square into nine equal-sized squares. Then remove the three squares in the middle column.

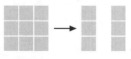

2. Suppose you modify the above iteration rule so that only one square, say the middle one, remains.

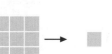

3. Suppose you modify the above iteration rule so that only the four corner squares remain.

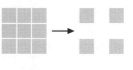

4. What if we keep the middle column of three squares, but remove the rest?

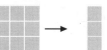

Here are several examples of fractals, each of which has been generated by a process of removals. In each case, we have used a square as the seed for the iteration rule. Give the iteration rule for each case (that is, what we remove at each stage) and draw the result of the first three iterations of this rule.

5. Note that this is not the Sierpiński triangle.

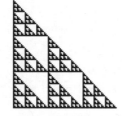

6. The Fractal T

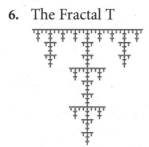

7. A plaid fractal

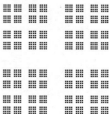

8. A fractal kite

9. You name this one.

Self-Similarity

OVERVIEW

This lesson introduces one of the formal properties of fractals: **self-similarity**. Students will become familiar with various ways of describing the concept of a ratio of similarity between successive iterations in the orbit. Phrases such as "applying a magnification factor of 2," "reducing by a scale factor of 2," and "applying a contraction factor of ½" are all used to describe rules for generating fractals. The real challenge appears when students are given a fractal and asked to determine: the magnification factor that was used to generate the fractal; what rotations, if any, were applied; and how many self-similar pieces appear in the image at any given level. Famous fractals included in this lesson are the Sierpiński triangle, the Koch curve, the Cantor middle-thirds set, and the Sierpiński carpet, along with a variety of less famous but very interesting fractals.

MATHEMATICAL PREREQUISITES

Students need to be familiar with the mathematical concepts of similarity, scale factors, 90° rotations, and exponents.

MATHEMATICAL CONNECTIONS

Topics from your mathematics curriculum that have connections to this lesson are **similarity**, **geometric transformations**, and **fractions** (particularly in Investigation 7). The Lesson Notes below and Answers in the back describe links to more specific concepts and skills.

TECHNOLOGY

A computer drawing program is useful in helping students visualize the "shrinking" of figures and the rotations. Most drawing programs allow you to shrink an image by varying percentages to simulate the reductions by ½, ⅓,

and so on. Most drawing programs also allow you to specify rotations. The Geometer's Sketchpad can perform all these transformations on a figure. Also, if you or your students have any background in programming in LOGO (students may have used this in elementary school), it is an excellent language for writing fractal generation programs because of its recursive structure and "turtle" drawing features.

SUGGESTED LESSON PLAN

CLASS TIME

One full 50-minute class period to work through the examples. Students can do the remaining problems outside of class.

PREPARATION

The teacher should read through the Explanation pages. The three transparencies aid in the presentation and discussion of the material. Remind students of the definition of similar polygons and what is meant by a ratio of similarity and scale factors. You might also want to discuss what happens to the ratio of the areas of similar figures when you magnify or contract their linear measurements, or you may prefer to have this discussion evolve naturally out of the lesson itself.

LESSON DEVELOPMENT

▵ Place Transparency 3A on the overhead (cover up the Fractal Plus example) and have students identify as many similar Sierpiński triangles as they can. If students are already familiar with ratios of similarity, use that to begin the discussion of magnification factors and contraction factors. (*Contraction factor* is the amount by which the image is reduced. *Magnification* is the amount by which a smaller self-similar image must be magnified to return to its original size.) Students tend to have difficulty distinguishing between linear dimensions and area if we simply say a figure is half as large. Make sure you point out that all magnifications and contractions are referring to linear measurements only.

▵ Ask students to identify magnification factors and/or contraction factors for various "sizes" of self-similar triangles within the Sierpiński triangle. Emphasize that a magnification factor of 3 means that the self-similar image you are looking at is $\frac{1}{3}$ the *linear* size of the original image.

⏶ Continue to have students identify self-similar copies and magnification factors from the Fractal Plus sign and rotation examples (Transparency 3B) and possibly identify the number of self-similar copies of a given "size."

⏶ If time allows, have students work on Investigations 1 and 2 in class. You might also include Further Exploration problem 1 if you want students to apply the rotation concepts.

LESSON NOTES

Again, be sure that students understand the "parallel" descriptions of dilations: magnifying a copy by a factor of 2 and applying a contraction factor of $\frac{1}{2}$ to the original. Mention that every time you magnify or "zoom in" on a fractal until you observe a smaller piece that is similar to the previous larger image, the following are true:

⏶ The linear measurements of the smaller piece are of $\frac{1}{s}$ times the corresponding measurements of the previous image, where s is the magnification factor.

⏶ The number of pieces congruent to the smaller piece increases by the same factor at every successive zoom.

INVESTIGATIONS

The first four investigations are fairly straightforward applications of the methods presented in the lesson. Investigations 5 and 6 are more challenging, with the latter involving some interesting work with fractions, comparison of fractions, and relative order of fractions. Investigations 1–4 do not involve rotations, while Investigation 5 and the Further Exploration problems do require an understanding of rotations.

Self-Similarity

The Sierpiński triangle:

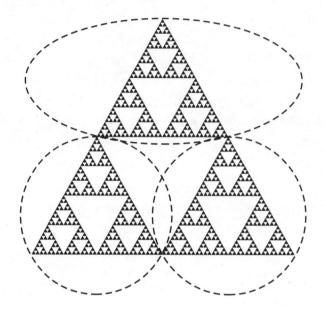

The Fractal Plus:

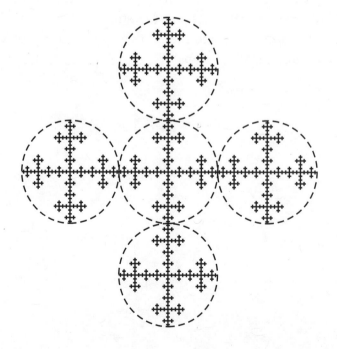

Rotations and Self-Similarity

Examine the following figure:

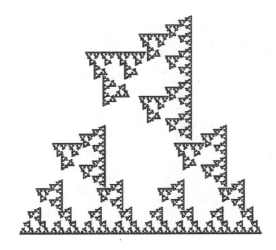

What's different from other fractals you have studied?

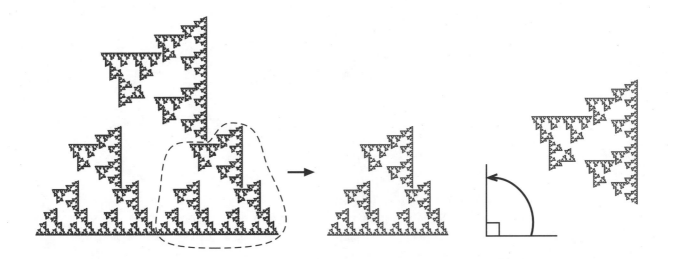

Just what is a fractal anyway? Clearly, objects like the Sierpiński triangle and carpet are very different from the typical objects in plane geometry. But what is it exactly that sets them apart from the familiar squares and triangles and circles of geometry? Actually, there are two important distinguishing features of fractals. The first is that fractals are **self-similar under magnification**. We will explain what this means in this lesson. The second property of fractals is that they have "fractional" dimension. We will describe what this means in another lesson.

In geometry, two figures are called similar if they have the same shape but are not necessarily the same size. For example, all equilateral triangles are similar. **Self-similarity** in a figure means that the overall shape of the figure is the same as the shape of a smaller part inside the figure, which in turn has the same shape as an even smaller part, which in turn has the same shape as an even smaller part, and so forth. The closer you look at a fractal, the more you see the same image.

THE SIERPIŃSKI TRIANGLE

Look more closely at the Sierpiński triangle below. Notice that it consists of three small copies of itself.

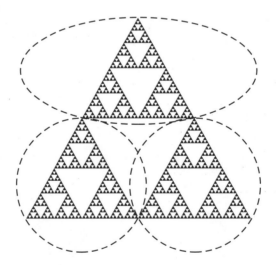

In fact, if you take a magnifying glass which magnifies the triangle by a factor of 2, and use it to look at any of the three regions circled above, what you see is an exact copy of the Sierpiński triangle. This is the idea of self-similarity under magnification: you can break up the Sierpiński triangle into three copies of itself, each of which may be magnified by a factor of 2 to yield the original figure. Each of these small pieces is called a **self-similar copy** of the Sierpiński triangle, and we say that each of them has **magnification factor** 2. Another way to say this is that the Sierpiński triangle consists of three self-similar pieces, each of which is one-half the size of the original. In this case, the number $\frac{1}{2}$ is a **contraction factor**.

This can be a little confusing. Sometimes we say that the self-similar copies can be magnified by a factor of 2 to yield the original, and other times we say that the original can be contracted by a factor of $\frac{1}{2}$ to yield the self-similar copies. Both mean the same thing. It's like saying that a yardstick is three times as long as a 12-inch ruler and a 12-inch ruler is one-third as long as a yardstick.

Incidentally, when we say "magnify by a factor of 2," we mean that the length and width of the figure is doubled. The area is thus multiplied by 4.

For the Sierpiński triangle, there is much more to the story. If you use a magnifying glass which magnifies by a factor of 4, you can find other smaller copies of the Sierpiński triangle more deeply embedded in the original figure. In fact, the Sierpiński triangle also consists of nine self-similar pieces, each of which may be magnified by a factor of 4 to yield the original triangle. Equivalently, each of these small pieces has sides one-fourth as long as those of the original triangle.

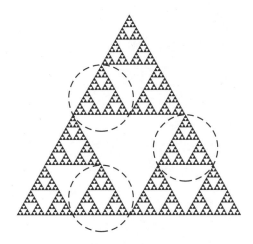

There is even more. Each of these nine smaller triangles consists of three more self-similar copies of the triangle, each of which is one-half the size of these pieces. So there are 27 small copies of the Sierpiński triangle embedded in the full figure, and each of these copies may be magnified by a factor of 8 to yield the entire figure.

There is a pattern here. The Sierpiński triangle consists of three self-similar pieces that each have magnification factor 2. It also consists of $9 = 3^2$ self-similar pieces that have magnification factor $4 = 2^2$. And it also consists of $27 = 3^3$ self-similar pieces with magnification factor $8 = 2^3$. If we continue examining smaller and smaller pieces of the Sierpiński triangle, we find that, at the nth stage, it consists of 3^n self-similar pieces that each have magnification factor 2^n. No matter how closely we look at this figure, we always find smaller and smaller copies of itself buried deep within.

We can also read off these numbers from the iteration rule that we used to construct the Sierpiński triangle in the first place. Recall that, given our initial triangle was a seed, we removed the middle triangle; this left us with three smaller triangles, each of which was exactly one-half the size of the original. At the second stage of the construction, we found nine smaller triangles that were each one-fourth the size of the original. And at the nth stage, we found 3^n triangles that were $\frac{1}{2}^n$ times the size of the original.

THE FRACTAL PLUS

Here is another fractal that we discussed in Lesson 2. You can find five self-similar copies of the entire image inside this picture. Don't forget the middle piece! Each of these copies is exactly one-third the size of the original figure. So the magnification factor for this fractal is 3.

If you magnify by a factor of 3 any of the regions inside the circles, you find another copy of the entire figure, so this fractal also consists of 5^2 self-similar pieces with magnification factor 3^2. Or zooming in even further, you find 5^n self-similar pieces with magnification factor 3^n.

ROTATIONS

Sometimes figures that are self-similar contain copies of themselves that must be rotated first and then later magnified to give an exact copy. For example, the following fractal consists of three self-similar pieces. The bottom two pieces of this image are exact copies of the whole image, but one-half the size.

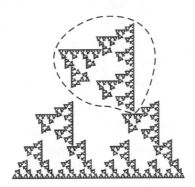

But the top piece of this fractal is an exact replica that seems to be rotated by 90° in the counterclockwise direction. To get this top piece of the fractal, we first shrink by a factor of 2:

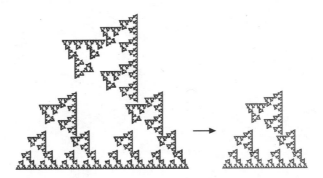

and then we rotate this piece by 90° in the counterclockwise direction:

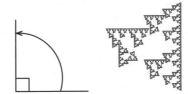

1 ▷ THE SIERPIŃSKI CARPET

We construct this figure by breaking up a square into nine smaller squares, with each side one-third the size of the original. Then we remove the middle square, leaving behind eight squares. At the same time, note that the carpet consists of eight self-similar pieces, each with a magnification factor of 3. If we zoom in toward any of these self-similar pieces using a magnification factor of 3, we see an exact copy of the carpet. So the Sierpiński carpet also consists of $64 = 8^2$ self-similar pieces, each with magnification factor $9 = 3^2$.

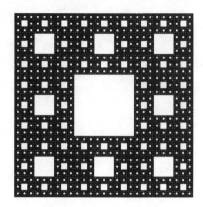

a. On this figure, find each self-similar piece that has magnification factor 3. Then fill in the appropriate column of the table below.

b. Find a piece of your fractal that demonstrates the fractal's self-similarity at a smaller scale. Record the magnification factor and the total number of pieces at this scale in the last column below.

Magnification factor	1	3	
Number of self-similar pieces	1		

2 ▷ THE SIERPIŃSKI HEXAGON

a. On this figure, find each self-similar piece that has magnification factor 3. Then fill in the appropriate column of the table below.

b. Find a piece of your fractal that demonstrates the fractal's self-similarity at a smaller scale. Record the magnification factor and the total number of pieces at this scale in the last column below.

Magnification factor	1	3	
Number of self-similar pieces	1		

3 ▷ THE FRACTAL T

a. On this figure, find each self-similar piece that has magnification factor 3. Then fill in the appropriate column of the table below.

b. Find a piece of your fractal that demonstrates the fractal's self-similarity at a smaller scale. Record the magnification factor and the total number of pieces at this scale in the last column below.

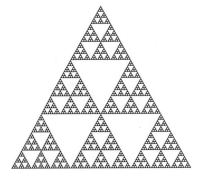

Magnification factor	1	3	
Number of self-similar pieces	1		

4 ▷ A RELATIVE OF THE SIERPIŃSKI TRIANGLE

a. On this figure, find each self-similar piece that has the smallest magnification factor. Then fill in the first blank column of the table below.

b. Find a piece of your fractal that demonstrates the fractal's self-similarity at a smaller scale. Record the magnification factor and the total number of pieces at this scale in the last column below.

Magnification factor	1		
Number of self-similar pieces	1		

5 ▷ THE KOCH CURVE

Here is a very famous fractal, the Koch curve, which we will explore in detail in Lesson 4.

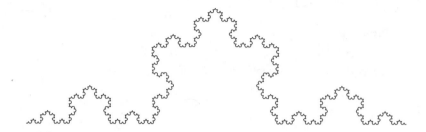

a. Are any of these self-similar pieces rotated? If so, by how much (approximately)?

_____

b. On this figure, find each self-similar piece that has the smallest magnification factor. Then fill in the first blank column of the table below.

c. Find a piece of your fractal that demonstrates the fractal's self-similarity at a smaller scale. Record the magnification factor and the total number of pieces at this scale in the last column below.

Magnification factor	1		
Number of self-similar pieces	1		

6 ▷ A FERN FRACTAL

So far, all of the figures that we have considered have been abstract geometric figures. Here is a picture that looks like something from the real world.

a. What can you say about the self-similarity of this figure?

_____

_____

_____

FRACTALS: A TOOL KIT OF DYNAMICS ACTIVITIES
©1999 KEY CURRICULUM PRESS

b. Can you think of other objects in the real world that exhibit self-similarity to some degree? List them here and explain how they are self-similar.

_____

_____

_____

7 ▷ THE CANTOR MIDDLE-THIRDS SET

To construct this set, take a segment and remove the middle third. Then remove the middle third from each of the two remaining segments. After removing middle thirds of the remaining segments forever, you obtain the Cantor middle-thirds set. This set is also a self-similar object.

a. Sketch a picture of this set and circle some of the self-similar regions. (*Hint:* Use a pencil to sketch the set so you can erase middle thirds of each segment.)

What is the corresponding magnification factor that matches the regions you circled?

_____

b. The Cantor middle-thirds set divides neatly into two pieces: one piece in the left-hand interval $0 \leq x \leq \frac{1}{3}$ and the other piece in the right-hand interval $\frac{2}{3} \leq x \leq 1$. Label the left endpoint of your Cantor set with the number 0 and the right endpoint with the number 1. Also label the appropriate points as $\frac{1}{3}$ and $\frac{2}{3}$.

c. For the moment, consider only the left-hand portion of the Cantor set. List at least eight different numbers that lie in this portion.

_____

_____

d. Now multiply each of these numbers by 3 and record the answer here:

_____

_____

e. Do each of these new numbers lie in the Cantor set? Do they all lie in the left-hand side of the Cantor set?

_____

_____

f. Take an endpoint of one of the intervals in the left side of the Cantor at the nth stage of its construction. What happens if you multiply it by 3?

_____

_____

g. Describe what you think of the following statement: Multiplication by 3 is a "magnifying glass" that magnifies the left portion of the Cantor set and yields the entire Cantor set.

_____

_____

h. Describe a similar magnifying glass that magnifies the left portion of the left side of the Cantor set (the portion in the interval $0 \leq x \leq \frac{1}{9}$) and yields the entire set.

_____

_____

i. How about the right portion of the interval $\frac{2}{3} \leq x \leq 1$? This is tougher. (Try to find an expression that maps 1 to 1 but $\frac{2}{3}$ to 0. There's a neat little hint for you!)

_____

_____

Describe the self-similarity of the following figures. Use a separate piece of paper. Be sure to answer all these questions for each figure:

⌂ How many self-similar copies of the original image can you find?

⌂ What are the magnification factors (approximately)? Are any copies rotated?

⌂ If copies are rotated, by how much? (Give an approximate answer. It is difficult to estimate the exact angle.)

1. 2. 3.

4. 5. 6. Warning: The last one is a toughie!

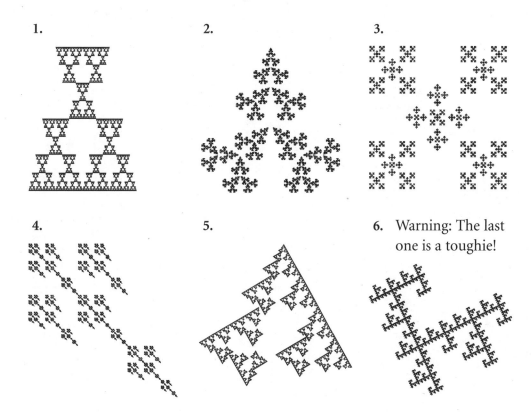

Copies of Copies

4

OVERVIEW

In this lesson, students learn yet another way to generate fractals geometrically. The "copies of copies" method involves making multiple copies of a reduced self-similar piece and arranging the copies according to a fixed rule. This is actually a primitive version of the method used by a number of fractal generation software programs. Students will revisit two of the famous fractals they may have worked with in previous lessons; however, it is not necessary that they have studied those lessons in order to work with the methods presented here. This activity also introduces the need for using directed line segments in fractal generation.

MATHEMATICAL PREREQUISITES

Students need to be familiar with the concepts of dilation (or "shrinking"), 180° rotations, 45°-45°-90° triangles, and perpendicular bisectors. (They need the last two concepts for Investigation 3 only, which could be omitted if these two topics are unfamiliar to students.)

MATHEMATICAL CONNECTIONS

Topics from your mathematics curriculum that have connections to this lesson are **geometric transformations** and **vectors**. The Lesson Notes below and Answers in the back describe links to more specific concepts and skills.

TECHNOLOGY

Computer drawing programs provide an excellent way to generate some of these iterations; see the Technology Tips in Investigations 1 and 2. Essentially any computer drawing program will work here, even the basic drawing program that comes with a word processing application. Investigations 4, 5, and 6 will look very much like LOGO procedures. If middle school students are familiar with

LOGO, then writing a LOGO procedure to produce the generator in these investigations would be a worthwhile geometric exercise. However, writing the program to continue the successive iterations is not trivial.

SUGGESTED LESSON PLAN

CLASS TIME

The entire activity probably requires two 50-minute class periods because it addresses a number of different fractal generations. Students will definitely need time to work with some of the rules on their own. One suggestion would be to present the Sierpiński examples and the "copy with a twist" on one day, using Investigations 1–3 for homework. Then on the second day develop the Koch curve and space-filling curve, both of which involve directed segments. You could then assign Investigations 4–6, and use Investigation 7 as a group classroom project.

PREPARATION

You will want to read through the Explanation pages yourself, but you may not need to copy them for students. If you wish to have students generate some of these images using a computer drawing program, you may need to make arrangements for computer time. In addition, you may need to arrange for the equipment to demonstrate how to generate the images in such a program. See the Technology Tips in the Investigations for suggested computer uses.

LESSON DEVELOPMENT

There are a number of ways to present this lesson. The following is one suggestion:

DAY 1

- Present the "copies of copies" approach by developing the Sierpiński triangle example on the first of the Explanation pages.

- Divide the class in half and have one group of students use the circle as their seed while the other group uses the stick figure. This can be done manually or with a computer drawing program if you have a computer lab available.

- Add the rotation piece before the end of class by using the "copies of copies with a twist" example at the end of the Explanation pages. Again, you could demonstrate this with a computer drawing program, or simply make a transparency of that page to show students the process.

⚬ Homework: Assign Investigations 1–3. (*Note:* Assign Investigation 3 only if students are familiar with a 45°-45°-90° triangle and perpendicular bisectors.) You could also assign Further Exploration problems 4 and 6 at this time. Problem 6 is designed as an extended project, but students could start it now and hand it in later.

DAY 2

⚬ After discussing the investigations students did for homework, present the Koch curve and the space-filling curve, both of which deal with directed segments.

⚬ Have students work on Investigation 4 in class to be sure they understand how to generate fractals with directed segments.

⚬ Have students read through Investigation 7. Assign different numbers between 0.25 and 0.5 to different students. (The purpose of these numbers is explained in the investigation.) Students should eventually work in groups so that each group has a series of different numbers among the group members in order to generate their "movie."

⚬ Homework: Assign Investigations 5 and 6 and any of the remaining Further Exploration problems for homework along with each student's own piece of Investigation 7.

LESSON NOTES

The problems in this section provide excellent opportunities both for cooperative group work and for using a computer graphics program.

INVESTIGATION 3

To complete this investigation, students need to be familiar with 45°-45°-90° triangles and perpendicular bisectors. If students are not familiar with these concepts, you could skip this Investigation, or you could introduce definitions at this time. They do not need to know all the relationships between the side lengths of the 45°-45°-90° triangle—simply that it is an isosceles right triangle.

FURTHER EXPLORATION, PROBLEM 7

For geometry students, an extension of this problem might be for them to calculate the actual perimeter of the first iteration (second image) and the area. Then have them do the same for the second iteration. See if they can describe the mathematical relationship between successive perimeters and successive areas.

If you studied Lesson 2 you learned how to produce fractals by removing designated parts of figures at each stage. Here we present a different way to construct fractals. This is the "copies of copies" construction. You begin with an initial seed—say, an equilateral triangle—and then make three copies reduced by 50%. Then you assemble the reduced copies as in the usual construction of the Sierpiński triangle.

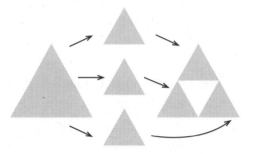

So the iteration rule is: "Copy three times at 50% reduction, then assemble." This rule is really the familiar Sierpiński triangle iteration, but stated in a slightly different way.

Now iterate. First make three copies of the new image at 50% reduction. Then assemble in the same way as before.

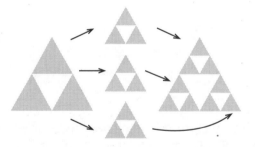

Clearly, this is just another way of generating the iteration rule for the Sierpiński triangle. Continuing this process yields our familiar fractal friend.

WHAT'S THE BIG DEAL?

Well, watch what happens when we use a different seed—say, a circle—but then use the same iteration rule. First copy three times. Then assemble.

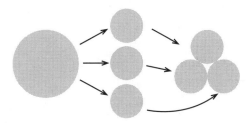

Do it again and again.

Do you see a familiar shape arising? Yes, it's the Sierpiński triangle!

Let's try this again. This time start with a stick figure. Make three copies, each reduced by 50%, then assemble, and then iterate:

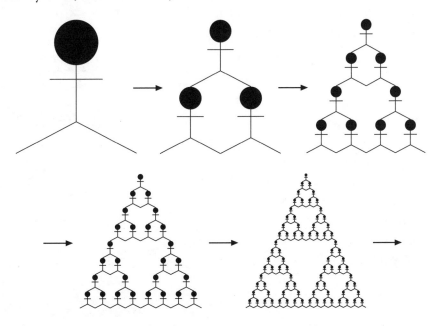

Again, we find that the limiting shape is the Sierpiński triangle.

COPIES OF COPIES WITH A TWIST

Suppose we add a slight twist to the "copies of copies" theme. Again, suppose we start with an equilateral triangle. As before we make three copies of the triangle at 50% reduction. Now, however, when we reassemble these triangles, we rotate the top triangle by 180° as in the figure at right.

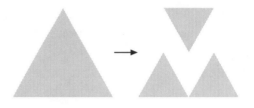

What happens when we iterate this rule? At the next stage, we make three copies, but when we reassemble, we must flip the top copy by 180°. The result is the figure at right.

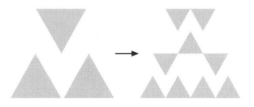

Notice that the bottom two pieces of this figure are the same as the previous image, only reduced by 50%. But the top piece has been reduced and then rotated by 180°. At the next stage, we do the same thing.

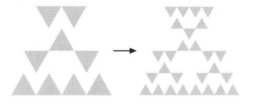

When this process is repeated over and over, another fractal image emerges. The image at right shows a later stage in the orbit begun above. The image is magnified so you can see more detail. Note that there are three self-similar copies. The two copies on the bottom are exact replicas of the entire fractal, only reduced by 50%. The top copy is also a reduced copy of the entire image, only rotated by 180°.

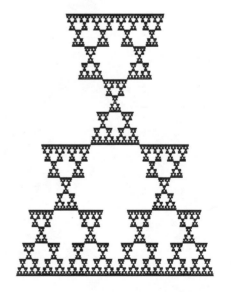

FRACTALS: A TOOL KIT OF DYNAMICS ACTIVITIES
©1999 KEY CURRICULUM PRESS

THE KOCH CURVE AND DIRECTED SEGMENTS

Here is another fractal generated by making copies of copies. Begin with a straight segment—say, with length 1. Make four copies of the segment, each reduced to ⅓ (that is, one-third the original size). Then reassemble as shown here.

The second figure is called the **generator** or the **initiator** for the iteration. Another way to think of this iteration is to remove the middle third of the given line segment and replace it with two segments, each of length equal to the length of the segment that was removed.

To iterate this rule, we simply replace each segment we encounter with a copy of the generator of the same size. That is, the next few images in the orbit are:

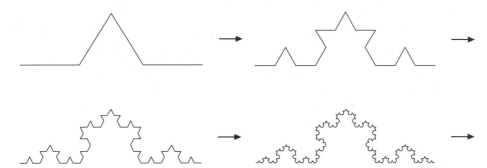

Continuing with this iteration rule, we eventually produce the Koch curve.

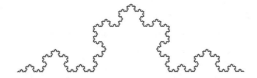

We will return to this fascinating Koch curve fractal over and over again.

The confusing part of this construction is determining which way to make the pointed bulge at each stage of the construction. In order to simplify this construction, we often use directed line segments to indicate which way the construction proceeds. For example, the iteration rule for the Koch curve may be written:

The arrows here indicate the direction we turn as we move along each segment of the construction. First we move in the same direction as the original segment. Then we turn to the left, then to the right. Finally, we continue in the same direction as the original segment, finishing exactly where the original segment ended.

A SPACE-FILLING CURVE

Making copies of copies can have surprising consequences when this type of iteration rule is carried out. For example, here is a very similar iteration rule. As before, we start with a line segment. We again make four copies, but this time each copy is half as long as the original. Then we assemble according to the following rule:

Despite appearances, there really are four segments here; the segment that is vertical has been covered twice. It is helpful to think about this process in terms of directed line segments. We start with a line segment heading to the right and replace it with four copies, each at 50% reduction: the first heading right, the second heading up, the third heading down, and the fourth heading right again.

FRACTALS: A TOOL KIT OF DYNAMICS ACTIVITIES
©1999 KEY CURRICULUM PRESS

When we iterate, we have to replace each of the line segments with a copy of the generator, and the new piece that pokes off the original segment must point to the left as we move in the direction of the arrow. That is, the next two images in this orbit are:

The four copies of the generator at the second stage in the orbit are shown here. Note that the projecting piece points leftward (in terms of our arrows) in each case.

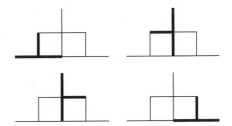

If we iterate this procedure, we find:

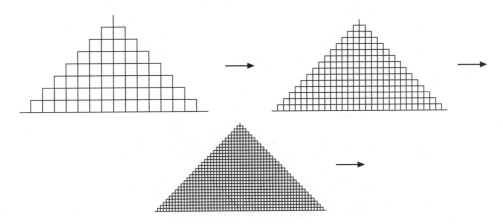

and we see that the orbit is approaching a triangle that is completely filled in.

1 ▷ TRIPLICATING A SQUARE

TECHNOLOGY TIP

Most computer drawing programs allow you to copy an object and scale it down. To scale several objects at once you may need to group them first.

Consider the following copying rule: Start with a square and make three copies of the square at 50% reduction.

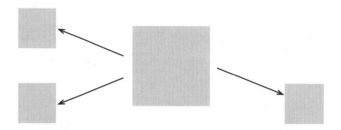

Then reassemble these squares like this:

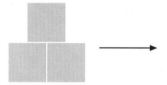

a. Sketch the next two iterations of this rule above.

b. What figure will result if you continue to iterate this rule?

2 ▷ TRIPLICATING WITH A TWIST

TECHNOLOGY TIP

Many computer drawing programs allow you to rotate objects as well as duplicating and scaling them. You may need to group the objects before you rotate them.

Suppose we make three copies of a figure, reduce each by 50%, and reassemble so that the top piece is rotated by 90° as shown below.

a. Sketch the next figure in this orbit.

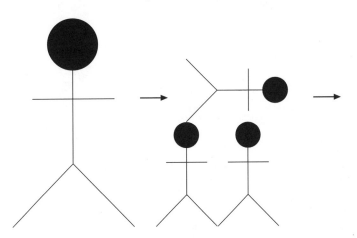

b. Describe the picture that will result when we iterate this rule many more times. (*Hint:* You may have seen this fractal in a previous lesson.)

_____

_____

3 ▷ DROP THE PERPENDICULAR

Describe the orbit generated by the following iteration rule. The seed is a 45°-45°-90° triangle. The iteration rule is to draw a perpendicular bisector to the side opposite the right angle, thereby producing two 45°-45°-90° triangles.

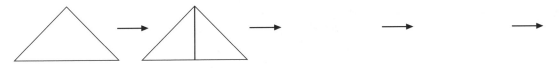

a. First, draw the next three figures in this orbit.

b. Then describe the figure that results when we iterate infinitely.

_____

_____

4 ▷ A SIERPIŃSKI SURPRISE

Here is a different iteration rule. Again we begin with a straight line segment. This time we make five copies of the line at 50% reduction. Then we arrange the lines as shown below.

This rule can be summarized as follows. Whenever we see a directed line segment, we add an equilateral triangle whose sides are each one-half the length of the original segment. The triangle is balanced on its tip. The next iteration therefore yields the picture at right.

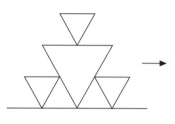

Note that the lower two small equilateral triangles are each traced twice in this process.

a. Draw the next iteration of this rule above.

b. Do you see a familiar pattern emerging? What is the fate of this orbit?

_____

_____

5 ▷ PARALLEL SEGMENTS

Now try this rule. Take a segment of length 1. Copy it three times at 50% reduction and put it down as shown below. Two of the copies lie along the original segment and the third is placed one-half unit above the original segment.

a. The bottom segment actually consists of two pieces lying end to end. Draw the next two iterations of this rule.

b. Again, what do you suspect will eventually appear as you iterate this rule?

_____

_____

6 ▷ THE HAT CURVE

A similar iteration rule appears here. Here the
middle third of any segment is replaced with a
"hat." As always, we need to know in which direction to draw the bulge.
That's why we replace the line segment with a directed line segment.

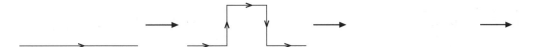

So the rule is: "Replace any line segment with one that has a hat pointing
leftward as you move along the segment."

a. Now draw the next two figures in this orbit. You do not need to show all the arrows.

b. Decide which of the following three fractals results when we continue this
iteration. This is not so easy.

i.   **ii.**   **iii.**

      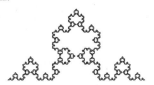

7 ▷ ANIMATING THE KOCH CURVE IN A FLIP BOOK

In this investigation you and your fellow students will collaborate to make a fractal movie. Each of you should choose a number between 0.25 and 0.5. Call this number a. This number is a factor that shows how much the segments shrink at each iteration. Each of you will construct the fractal given by the iteration rule shown here. Notice that the original segment has length 1 and the segments at the next iteration have length $a \cdot 1$.

You obtain the Koch curve when $a = \frac{1}{3}$, and a space-filling curve when $a = \frac{1}{2}$.

a. First draw the next three figures in your orbit, using your particular value of a. Make sure that you all start with a segment of the same length.

b. Then, on a separate sheet draw the sixth figure in this orbit.

c. When all of your classmates are finished, collect results from (b) and order them according to their a-values. To animate your results as frames of a movie, attach one edge of the pages together to make a flip book. (*Note:* Flip books often work better with stiff paper and smaller images.)

1. For this next rule, we begin with a line segment of length 1. Make 3 copies of it at 50% reduction, and arrange them as shown here: two of the copies lie along the original segment; the third is perpendicular to and bisects the original segment. Now iterate this process.

   a. First draw the next three iterations.

   b. Then determine which of the following three fractals is the result of this process.

   i.   ii.   iii.

   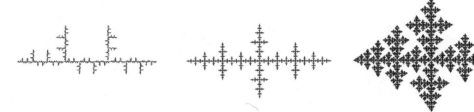

For each of the fractals in problems 2–4:

   a. Sketch the generator used to construct each fractal.

   b. Describe the copying rule that was used to generate the fractal.

   c. If possible, test your answers by regenerating each image using technology.

2.   3.   4.

     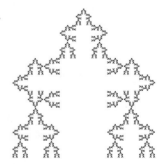

5. Determine the fractal that results if we iterate the following copying rule: Start with a segment of length 1. Then make two copies of this segment at $\frac{1}{3}$ the length of the original. Then place the two segments down as follows:

6. What fractal results if we start with a regular hexagon, make six copies with sides ⅓ the length of the original, then arrange the copies at the vertices of a regular hexagon?

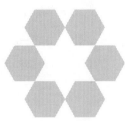

7. A famous image related to the Koch curve is known as the Koch snowflake curve. Basically, the snowflake is obtained by performing the same iteration rule as produced the Koch curve, but using a seed that is a triangle rather than the straight line. Here are the first two steps in this construction.

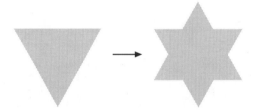

   a. Continue iterating on the second image above and create your own image of the Koch snowflake.

   b. Do some research about the Koch snowflake's area and perimeter. What is remarkable about the area and perimeter of this shape?

TECHNOLOGY TIP

You can use a photocopy machine to duplicate and reduce a picture. Try not to waste paper!

8. Choose any picture whatsoever as your seed. You might create your own image by hand or on a computer, or cut one from a magazine. Then create three copies of your picture at 50% reduction. Reassemble your three copies in triangular form as in Investigation 1. Continue to iterate this rule, creating and arranging more and more smaller copies of the previous image. Organize your results as a poster and describe your work. Include your prediction of what you think will result if you continue to iterate this rule indefinitely.

TEACHER NOTES

Random Iteration: The Chaos Game

OVERVIEW

In this lesson, students are introduced to the chaos game. This is different from the geometric iteration methods in Lessons 2–4 because this fractal generation process is random and not deterministic. You or your students may have seen this game before, as it is one of the more popular introductions to the mathematical topics of chaos and fractals. However, you will see some new twists here, including a version students can play at our Web site and some assistance with the formulas needed for programming a calculator to play this game.

MATHEMATICAL PREREQUISITES

In addition to being familiar with basic geometric shapes, students will need to be fairly well versed in coordinate geometry, including creating formulas for the midpoints of segments. This work with coordinates, however, occurs only in the optional section on programming a calculator.

MATHEMATICAL CONNECTIONS

Topics from your mathematics curriculum that have connections to this lesson are **measurement**, **probability**, **coordinates**, **logic**, and **problem solving**. The Lesson Notes below and Answers in the back describe links to more specific concepts and skills.

TECHNOLOGY

It is very helpful for students to see the results of the chaos game after a large number of iterations, and technology can do this accurately and efficiently. A version of the chaos game is available for students to play on our Web site. The address of this site is **http://math.bu.edu/DYSYS/applets/fractalina.html**. This Web site is Java-enhanced and contains interactive fractal demonstrations and Java software. Java is a cutting-edge technology that allows you to run programs (called "Java applets") directly from the Internet. You won't need to download or install these programs before use; they're downloaded automatically when you visit a Java-enhanced Web site. However, in order to access them, you'll need an Internet connection and a "Java-enhanced Web browser." Because Java is new, only recent versions of Web browser programs are likely to support it. (If you use Netscape Navigator or Microsoft Internet Explorer, Version 3 was the first version to support Java.) Even if you have a recent browser, it may not be configured to run Java programs automatically. Check your browser's Preferences or Options dialog, or talk to your network systems administrator, to verify that Java is supported and enabled.

Students may also want to create their own chaos game on a programmable calculator or on a computer. For this reason the mathematical formulas needed to write such a program are derived in the Explanation pages of this lesson. Also, check the guidebook of your graphing calculator. Many contain the program steps for a simple version of the chaos game.

SUGGESTED LESSON PLAN

CLASS TIME

One 50-minute class period to play the standard chaos game without technology. An additional period would be needed if you have access to computers for students to play the game at our Web site.

PREPARATION

Teachers should read through the Explanation pages on how to play the game and why the game results in the image of the Sierpiński triangle. Make copies of Investigation 1 for students. It works well to have students work in pairs, where one student rolls the die and the other records the points on the worksheet, so you only need one copy for each pair of students. Also have four or five overhead transparencies ready onto which students can trace their points after they have accumulated 15–20 points beyond the initial 6 which they erase. Several pairs of students can record their points on the same transparency. (Make sure the transparencies have the three vertices already on them to match up with the Investigation 1 worksheets.) You may also want to run off copies of the halfway ruler ahead of time for students to use. Although the rulers can be copied on regular paper, they are easier to use if run either on card stock or on transparencies, with several rulers to one sheet of paper to be cut apart. You could also have students draw their own ruler.

If you can use our Web site's chaos game with students, make sure you have tried to access it from your lab ahead of time.

LESSON DEVELOPMENT

DAY 1

▲ Introduce the rules for the chaos game and hand out the materials needed to play: copies of Investigation 1, dice, and halfway rulers (or regular rulers). If you are short on time, have students work directly on the transparencies. Make sure not to tell them what the final image is, and don't distribute any pages with images of the Sierpiński triangle yet.

▲ As students complete a sufficient number of points, circulate four or five transparencies and overhead marker pens around the room so students can record their points on the transparencies. Vertices that align with the Investigation 1 worksheet must be on the transparencies already. (*Note:* If you make the transparencies on a photocopy machine, be sure to run them from the master you used to create the student sheets—not from a student copy. Most photocopy machines reduce the image ever so slightly, so you want your transparency image to be reduced the same amount as the student pages—or the vertices will not line up when you overlay them.)

▲ As all "games" are recorded, overlay the transparencies on the overhead projector. Students should be able to see the image of the Sierpiński triangle beginning to take shape. At the very least, they should realize that the middle section of the triangle is not being filled in. Then show them the "real thing"— by accessing the Web site, by running some simulations using other technology, or by using Transparencies 5A and 5B.

▲ Demonstrate how to play the game with the triangle showing (Investigation 2), using Transparency 5C. Then use the second part of the transparency to figure out a "target practice" problem. One sequence of rolls that will hit this particular target is 4, 6, 1, 1, 5.

▲ Homework: Assign Investigations 2–5.

DAY 2

▲ Answer any questions from the Investigations.

▲ Have students play the chaos game from the Web site, if possible. If you do not have Web access, perhaps a student or another teacher can set up a computer or calculator program. (See Further Exploration problems 6 and 7.)

LESSON NOTES

Trying to develop a strategy for the chaos game target practice is an excellent problem-solving challenge in recognizing patterns. Investigations 2 and 3 are designed to help students begin to build that strategy. The version of this game that is available at the Web site challenges students to hit the target in the smallest possible number of moves, which can be done every time once they figure out the strategy.

The section of the Explanation pages on coordinate formulas for the chaos game is there primarily to assist in designing a program. However, an excellent challenge for students in an algebra or geometry class might be to attempt to *derive* the formulas developed here; they will probably need some initial guidance or hints unless you have an accelerated class. *Note:* Further Exploration problem 5 is a follow-up to this formula development. You will want to skip this problem if you are not planning on working with the coordinate formulas.

The Chaos Game

After 300 Iterations:

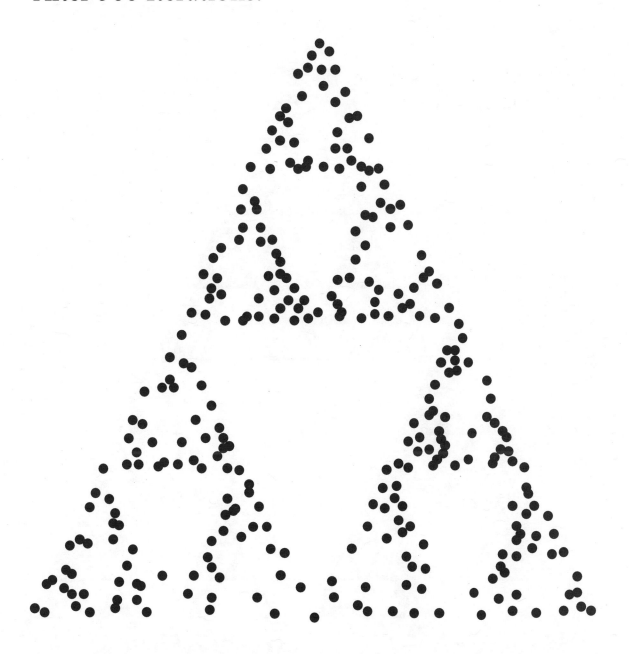

The Chaos Game

After 150,000 Iterations (on a computer using smaller dots):

FRACTALS: A TOOL KIT OF DYNAMICS ACTIVITIES
©1999 KEY CURRICULUM PRESS

The Chaos Game on the Sierpiński Triangle

Roll 1, 3, 5. Where do
you land?

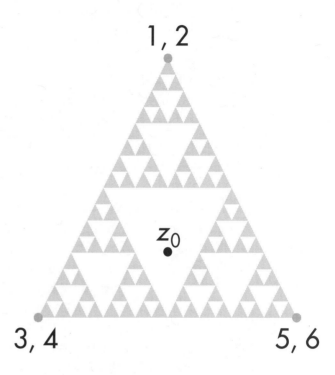

Find a sequence of
rolls that land the dot
on the shaded target.

Rolls _____ , _____ ,

_____ , _____ , _____ ,

_____ , _____ , _____ ,

_____ , _____ , _____

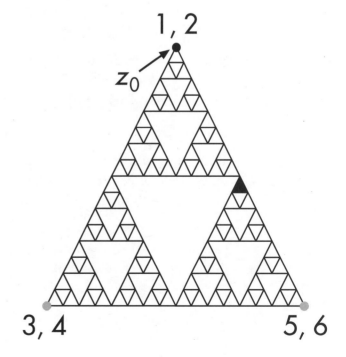

In this section we describe a type of geometric iteration known as the **chaos game**. Unlike previous geometric iterations you may have used to build geometric shapes, the steps in this process will be random. However, the result that we find will be anything but random.

To start playing the game, place three points at the vertices of a triangle. Call the first point "1, 2"; call the second point "3, 4"; and call the third point "5, 6." The reason for this strange notation is that you will use the roll of a die to select one of these three vertices during the iteration. For example, if you roll a 1 or a 2, then you select the vertex labeled "1, 2."

To begin the iteration, you need a seed. The seed in this case will be a point in the plane. For the seed you may choose any point in the interior of the triangle. Call this point z_0. Now the iteration rule is this: First roll the die to determine a vertex; then, depending on which number comes up, move to a new point z_1 which is exactly halfway between z_0 and the target vertex. For example, if you roll a 2, you move to the point z_1 that is located halfway between z_0 and the vertex marked "1, 2."

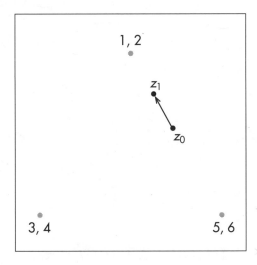

Now continue in this way. The next point z_2 is located halfway between z_1 and the vertex determined by the next roll of the die. For example, if the chosen triangle is the one in the figure at the right with z_0 as shown, then successive rolls of 1, 3, and 6 would yield the orbit shown on the right.

The question that arises is: What pattern emerges if we play this game thousands and thousands of times?

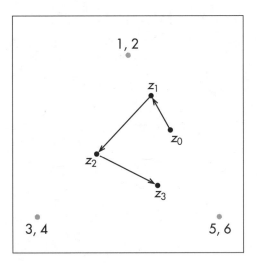

FRACTALS: A TOOL KIT OF DYNAMICS ACTIVITIES
©1999 KEY CURRICULUM PRESS

THE HALFWAY RULER

To help you make these moves accurately, you should first make a "halfway ruler." This is a wonderful little invention of a mathematics and art teacher from Boston named Henri Lion. Take a piece of paper and copy the following ruler onto its edge.

For each move, align this ruler so that the initial point and the target vertex are located at equal positions on opposite sides of the halfway point on the ruler. For example, if you start at z_2 and roll a 5, then you land on z_3 as shown here.

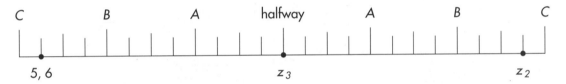

PLAYING THE GAME

The question that arises is: What image will emerge if you roll the die thousands and thousands of times and record the orbit? In order to make sure that you truly have a random process, whenever you play the game, it helps if you erase the first 10 or so points in the orbit. That way, you will begin recording the orbit at a more random seed.

Most people think that, since the game is entirely random, the picture of the orbit should be a "random mess." Some people think that the orbit should fill the entire triangle; others think the orbit will be a "formless blob" in the middle of the triangle. Before reading any further you should now try Investigation 1 in this lesson to see how your version of the chaos game unfolds.

After playing the chaos game with 150 iterations (and removing the first 10 points in the orbit), we obtained the following picture.

Clearly, the orbit does not enter certain parts of the triangle. There is a large triangular region in the middle of the original triangle that seems to be vacant. Around this triangle are three smaller vacant regions, and other still smaller vacant regions. . . . Wait a minute—we have seen this structure before. The orbit is beginning to resemble the Sierpiński triangle! Here is the same orbit, this time with 300 iterations.

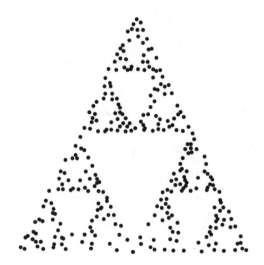

The Sierpiński triangle is even more evident here. Below is the result of 150,000 iterations done by computer and with tinier dots:

WHY, WHY, WHY?

At first, it seems amazing that something geometrically regular can emerge from a purely random game. In fact, we will see in the next few lessons that fractal images often arise in this way. Before turning to other versions of the chaos game, however, let's figure out why the Sierpiński triangle is the result of this random iteration.

Suppose you had started with a seed z_0 right in the middle of the largest central (missing) triangle. Remember that you erase z_0 in the chaos game; that's why you don't see z_0 in the final picture.

Now what happens when you begin the iteration? Well, z_1 is located halfway between z_0 and one of the three vertices, so z_1 must land in one of the three smaller white triangles at the next level of the construction. Use your halfway ruler to check.

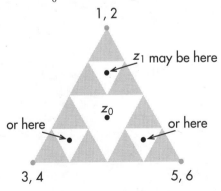

But remember that you erase z_1, so you don't see a dot at this second level in the final picture.

Now iterate one more time. The point z_2 moves into the next smaller white triangle in the picture. For example, suppose z_0 and z_1 are as shown:

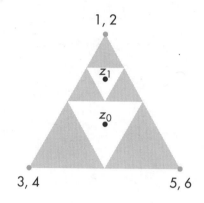

Then z_2 must lie in one of the three small triangles as shown at the right.

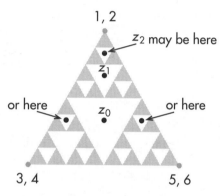

TECHNOLOGY TIP

To understand this even better, play the on-line chaos game at the following Web site:

http://math.bu.edu/DYSYS/applets/chaos-game.html

As another example, if you begin in the center of the middle missing triangle and roll a 4 and then a 6, you would end up in the triangles shown at the right.

Again we see that at each stage of the iteration the orbit hops into a triangle of the next smaller size.

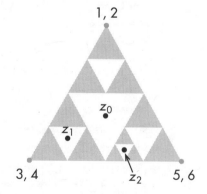

If instead we roll 4, 6, 1, we see a similar pattern.

So we see that each time we roll the die, our point moves into smaller and smaller missing triangles. Eventually, the point moves into microscopically small triangles that are not visible to the human eye. Although the point is still inside a missing triangle, it is getting closer and closer to shaded triangles. The point is slowly being attracted to the Sierpiński triangle, the region consisting only of gray points. For this reason, the Sierpiński triangle is often called the **attractor** of the chaos game. Any orbit is eventually attracted to this image.

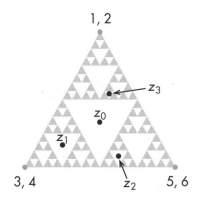

NONRANDOM ROLLS

The Sierpiński triangle results only if the rolls of the die are random. If this is not the case, then the results of the chaos game can be very different. For example, if you always rolled a 1, then no matter where you began, your orbit would be a sequence of points tending to the vertex marked "1, 2."

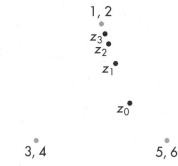

FORMULAS FOR THE CHAOS GAME

In case you would like to write a program to automate the chaos game on a computer or programmable calculator, you need to know the mathematical formulas that govern the three possible moves in the chaos game. For simplicity, let's assume that we have chosen our vertices on a right triangle. Say the vertices are $(0, 0)$, $(1, 0)$, and

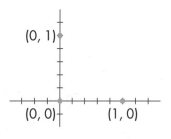

$(0, 1)$. We need to derive a formula that takes a given point (x_0, y_0) in the plane to a new point (x_1, y_1) located half the distance from one of these vertices.

The case for vertex $(0, 0)$ is easiest. To move $\left(x_0, y_0\right)$ half the distance to the origin, we simply halve both the x- and y-coordinates. That is, the formulas for this move are:

$$x_1 = \tfrac{1}{2}x_0$$

$$y_1 = \tfrac{1}{2}y_0$$

For example, if our point is located at $\left(\tfrac{1}{3}, \tfrac{1}{3}\right)$ in the plane, we move to $\left(\tfrac{1}{6}, \tfrac{1}{6}\right)$ when the origin is the selected vertex.

If we choose either of the other two vertices, the formulas change slightly. For example, to move half the distance to $(1, 0)$, we still take half of the y-coordinate, but now we must average the two x-coordinates to find the x-coordinate midway between. That is, these formulas are:

$$x_1 = \tfrac{1}{2}\left(x_0 + 1\right)$$

$$y_1 = \tfrac{1}{2}y_0$$

Similarly, to move half the distance to $(0, 1)$, the formulas are:

$$x_1 = \tfrac{1}{2}x_0$$

$$y_1 = \tfrac{1}{2}\left(y_0 + 1\right)$$

For example, if you are located at the point $\left(\tfrac{1}{2}, \tfrac{1}{2}\right)$ and select the lower right vertex $(1, 0)$, the new point is given by:

$$x_1 = \tfrac{1}{2}\left(x_0 + 1\right) = \tfrac{1}{2}\left(\tfrac{1}{2} + 1\right) = \tfrac{3}{4}$$

$$y_1 = \tfrac{1}{2}x_0 = \tfrac{1}{2} \cdot \tfrac{1}{2} = \tfrac{1}{4}$$

If you now select the vertex $(0, 0)$, the next new point is given by:

$$x_2 = \tfrac{1}{2}\left(x_1\right) = \tfrac{1}{2}\left(\tfrac{3}{4}\right) = \tfrac{3}{8}$$

$$y_2 = \tfrac{1}{2}x_1 = \tfrac{1}{2} \cdot \tfrac{1}{4} = \tfrac{1}{8}$$

1 ▷ PLAYING THE GAME

In the following diagram, play the chaos game with the given vertices. Play with a partner. One of you should roll the die and the other should plot the points and record them. Follow the rules as described on the first page of this lesson or by your teacher. You should choose z_0 somewhere inside the triangle. Then, using your halfway ruler and *pencil*, plot the first seven points—z_0, z_1, z_2, z_3, z_4, z_5, and z_6—determined by your die rolls. Remember to plot the points very accurately.

1, 2

3, 4   5, 6

After plotting z_6, switch to a *pen* and plot z_7, z_8, . . . , z_{15} on the same figure above. Once you have done this, erase z_0, z_1, z_2, z_3, z_4, z_5, and z_6.

a. Describe any pattern at this stage.

_____

b. Compare your results with those of your classmates. Describe how your patterns compare to theirs.

_____

_____

Continue to plot the next 20 or so points in the orbit using pen. Then, if transparencies are available, copy the vertices of the original triangle and the points of your orbit onto a transparency while the rest of the class does the same. Do not label the points on the transparency. Bring it up to the overhead projector and put yours in the pile with the rest. Make sure that the vertices of the outside triangle on your transparency lines up with those on the other transparencies.

c. Describe any pattern you see now.

_____

_____

_____

Simulate the chaos game using technology if you can. This way you can see the results of many, many iterations quickly.

d. Describe the patterns you see after hundreds of iterations.

_____

_____

_____

TECHNOLOGY TIP

You can use the simulation Fractalina on the Web at the address below. Press the Start button to run the simulation.

http://math.bu.edu/DYSYS/applets/fractalina.html.

2 ▷ PLAYING THE GAME WITH THE SIERPIŃSKI TRIANGLE SHOWING

Suppose z_0 lies in the center of the middle missing triangle. Suppose you now play the chaos game and your three rolls of the die are the ones indicated. Plot the corresponding orbit points z_1, z_2, and z_3 in each picture below.

a. You roll 1, 3, 5.

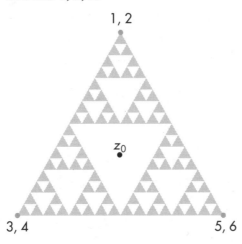

b. You roll 6, 6, 1.

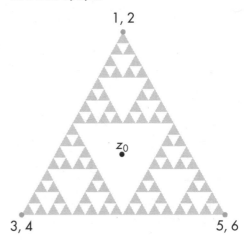

c. You roll 5, 3, 5.

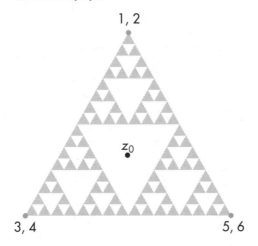

3 ▷ TARGET PRACTICE

TECHNOLOGY TIP

You can play a very similar target practice game at the Web site
http://math.bu.edu/DYSYS/applets/chaos-game.html.

In each of the figures below, suppose you start with z_0 in the center of the middle white triangle. What rolls of the die are necessary in each case for you to land in the shaded target triangles after *two* iterations?

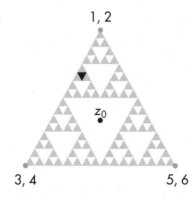

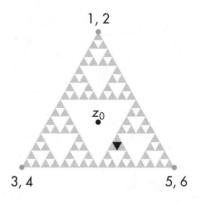

a.

Die rolls: _____

b.

Die rolls: _____

In each of the figures below, suppose you again start with z_0 in the center of the middle white triangle. What rolls of the die in each case will allow you to land in the shaded target triangles after *three* iterations?

c.

Die rolls: _____

d.

Die rolls: _____

4 ▷ NONRANDOM CHAOS GAMES

If the rolls of your die are not truly random, the orbit need not fill up the Sierpiński triangle.

a. Can you predict what would happen if you alternately rolled: 1, 3, 1, 3, 1, 3, . . . ? Sketch the orbit and describe its fate.

1, 2

z_0

3, 4   5, 6

_____

_____

_____

_____

_____

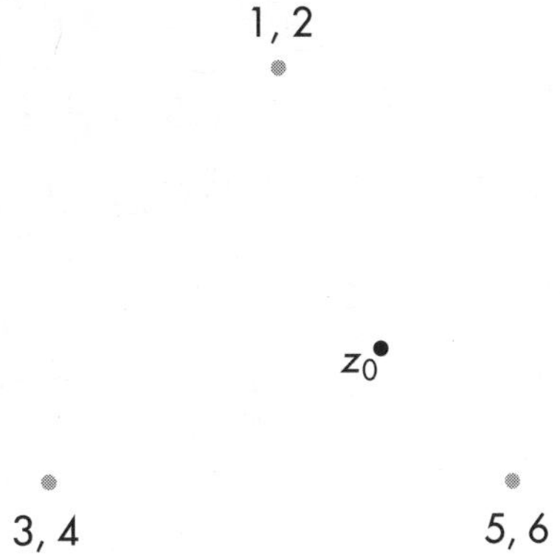

b. How about 1, 6, 1, 6, 1, 6, . . . ? Sketch the orbit and describe its fate.

1, 2

z_0

3, 4   5, 6

_____

_____

_____

_____

_____

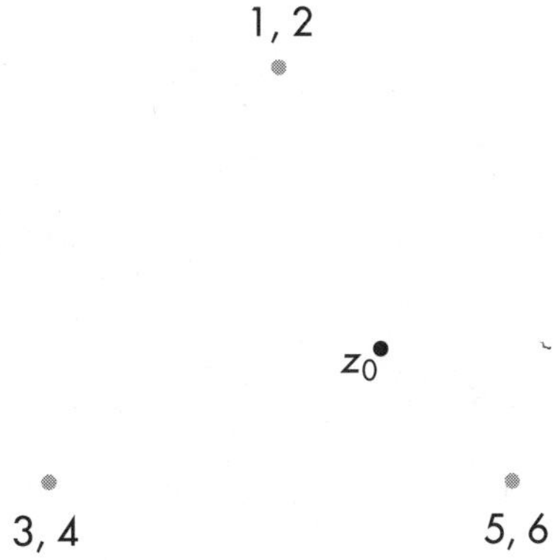

c. How about 2, 4, 6, 2, 4, 6, 2, 4, 6, . . . ? Sketch the orbit and describe its fate.

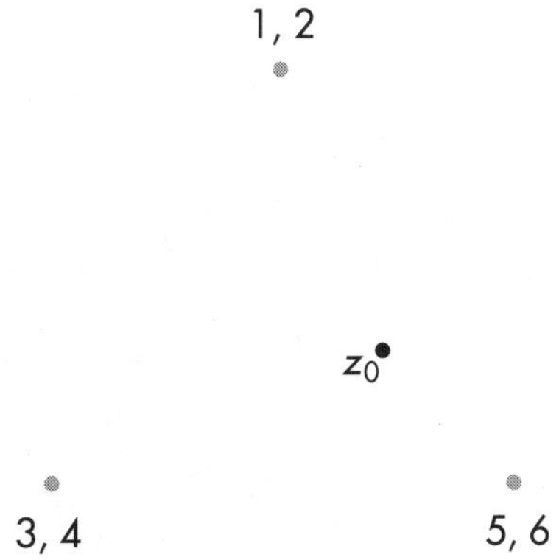

1, 2

z_0

3, 4   5, 6

_____

_____

_____

_____

_____

5 ▷ ANOTHER CHAOS GAME

Let's now play a different chaos game. Instead of playing the game in a triangle, we will play it in the interval $0 \leq x \leq 1$. Instead of using three vertices, we will use only two, one located at 0 and the other located at 1. Finally, rather than using a die to determine the random orbits, we will instead flip a coin. So we call the vertex at 0 "H" for heads and the vertex at 1 "T" for tails.

The rules of this new game are as follows: Choose a seed anywhere in the interval $0 \leq x \leq 1$. Flip the coin. If the coin turns up heads, then move the point toward the vertex marked H so that the new distance to H is exactly $\frac{1}{3}$ of the old distance. If the coin turns up tails, move the point so that the new distance from T is exactly $\frac{1}{3}$ of the old distance. For example, if you are initially located at $\frac{1}{2}$ and heads turns up, you move to the point $\frac{1}{6}$; but if tails turns up, you move to the point $\frac{5}{6}$.

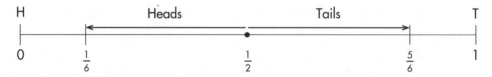

a. Starting at the indicated point, sketch the orbit of this point if the coin came up H, H, T in succession:

b. Starting at the indicated point, sketch the position of the orbit if the coin came up H, T, H, T in succession:

c. Starting at $\frac{1}{2}$, list the exact positions of the orbit if the coin came up H, H, T in succession: _____

d. Starting at $\frac{1}{4}$, list the exact positions of the orbit if the coin came up T, H, T, H, T, H, ... _____

e. Suppose your point is located at position x in the interval $0 \leq x \leq 1$ and the coin turns up H. Give a formula for your new position. _____

FRACTALS: A TOOL KIT OF DYNAMICS ACTIVITIES
©1999 KEY CURRICULUM PRESS

f. Suppose your point is located at position x in the interval $0 \leq x \leq 1$ and the coin turns up T. Give a formula for your new position. _____

If you begin at an arbitrary point in the interval $0 \leq x \leq 1$ and the coin turns up H, then your new position must be in the interval $0 \leq x \leq \frac{1}{3}$. On the other hand, if the coin turns up T, then your new position is somewhere in the interval $\frac{2}{3} \leq x \leq 1$. We can indicate these allowed positions as in this figure:

g. Indicate on this axis the possible positions to which an arbitrary point would move under successive appearances of HT (first heads, then tails), HH, TH, and TT:

h. Indicate below the possible positions corresponding to all possible combinations of *three* coin flips:

TECHNOLOGY TIP

Play the Web simulation Fractalina, but use two points and compression factors of 3. The URL for this site is:

http://math.bu.edu/DYSYS/applets/fractalina.html.

When we played the chaos game with three vertices, our traveling point traced out the Sierpiński triangle.

If you were to play this chaos game with many thousands of flips, what object would you expect your traveling point to move toward? (If possible, run a simulation using a computer or a calculator to test your prediction.)

1. Explain in your own words why the chaos game played on three vertices generates the Sierpiński triangle. Use diagrams to illustrate your explanation.

2. When you began the chaos game, you chose a seed that lies inside the triangle. Was this necessary? What would happen if you started with a seed outside of this triangle?

3. Instead of playing the chaos game with vertices on an equilateral triangle, suppose we start with the vertices of a right triangle. What figure results when we play the chaos game with these vertices?

4. What rolls of the die are necessary to hit the shaded targets below using the given seed? You must hit the interior of the target, not the boundary of it. Use as few rolls of the die as possible.

a.

1, 2

3, 4   seed   5, 6

b.

1, 2   seed

3, 4   5, 6

5. a. What is the formula for moving a point (x, y) half the distance to the point whose coordinates are $(2, 3)$?

   b. What is the formula for moving a point (x, y) half the distance to the point whose coordinates are (a, b)?

6. Play the chaos game at the Web site **http://math.bu.edu//DYSYS/applets/ chaos-game.html**. Find a strategy that guarantees you the best score for every game. Describe your strategy and how you came up with it. (Look ahead to Lesson 11 if you need hints.)

7. Program a calculator or a computer to run a simulation of one of the games in this lesson.

Other Chaos Games

OVERVIEW

This lesson deals with chaos game variations. Students see that a slight change in the rules of the game yields very different results. You will want to access the Web site referred to below or obtain another commercial software product in order to get the most out of this lesson.

MATHEMATICAL CONNECTIONS

Students need to be familiar with basic geometric shapes such as triangles and hexagons. In addition, they will need some knowledge of coordinate geometry and 30°-60°-90° triangle relationships (or the Pythagorean theorem) in order to complete Further Exploration problems 2 and 3. Students should be somewhat familiar with the preceding lesson, Random Iteration: The Chaos Game.

MATHEMATICAL PREREQUISITES

Topics from your mathematics curriculum that have connections to this lesson are **probability**, **measurement**, **number sense**, **spatial visualization**, **problem solving**, **pattern recognition**, and **symmetry**, as well as **coordinate geometry** in Further Exploration problems 2 and 3. The Lesson Notes below and Answers in the back describe links to more specific concepts and skills.

TECHNOLOGY

It is extremely desirable that you have software that can play these altered chaos games. A random number generator on either a calculator or computer would also be useful (see the five-vertices example in the Explanation pages). Further Exploration problem 4 suggests writing a program for a calculator or computer to simulate the game for six vertices and a compression factor of 3. This requires some fairly complicated algebraic formulas, which are outlined

in the answers to Further Exploration problems 2 and 3, and would provide a challenging activity for upper level students.

Students can play any version of the chaos game described in this activity on our Web site. The address of this site is **math.bu.edu/DYSYS/applets/ fractalina.html**. This Java-enhanced Web site contains interactive fractal demonstrations and Java software. Java is a cutting-edge technology that allows you to run programs (called "Java applets") directly from the Internet. You won't need to download or install these programs before use; they're downloaded automatically when you visit a Java-enhanced Web site. However, in order to access them, you'll need an Internet connection and a "Java-enhanced Web browser." Because Java is so new, only recent versions of Web browser programs are likely to support it. (If you use Netscape Navigator or Microsoft Internet Explorer, Version 3 was the first version to support Java.) Even if you have a recent browser, it may not be configured to run Java programs automatically. Check your browser's Preferences or Options dialog, or talk to your network systems administrator, to verify that Java is supported and enabled.

SUGGESTED LESSON PLAN

CLASS TIME

One or two 50-minute class periods, depending on the accessibility of technology—in particular, access to the Web site.

PREPARATION

If students did not see the preceding lesson, Random Iteration: The Chaos Game, then you need to play the basic chaos game with them from that lesson before introducing these alternative versions. If you don't have Web access or can't get the Java applets to operate, you may want to make copies of the Explanation pages for students, or put the images of some of the examples on overhead transparencies to share with them.

LESSON DEVELOPMENT

▵ Begin by reminding students of the rules in the original chaos game (Lesson 5). Ask students how they think the resulting image would be affected if you altered the compression factor in the chaos game. Ideally, you would then demonstrate that effect by playing this new game on the Web site using "Fractalina." If Web-site access is not possible at this time, use Transparency 6A to help students visualize the effect.

▲ Go through the other games from the Explanation pages by asking students to predict the outcome, then actually playing the game with "Fractalina" or one of the alternative software products. Again, if the software is not available, you may need to create transparencies for these other examples.

▲ Have students work through the Investigations using the Web site. If this is not an option, students could do Investigations 6 and 7 as well as Further Exploration problem 1 without the software—although they will find these problems more difficult if they have not had the opportunity to build a "feel" for these games from actually playing some of them.

▲ Homework options would come from the Investigations and Further Exploration problems that do not require the software (as suggested in the previous bulleted item). If students can access the Web applets outside of class, you can assign other problems as well.

LESSON NOTES

As mentioned above, all activities with the exception of Investigations 6 and 7 and Further Exploration problem 1 are fairly dependent on the chaos game software to be effective.

Further Exploration problems 2 and 3 require some sophisticated algebraic manipulation of coordinate geometry and provide excellent extended activities for capable geometry or advanced algebra classes.

Other Chaos Games

The original game: Three vertices, compression factor 2.

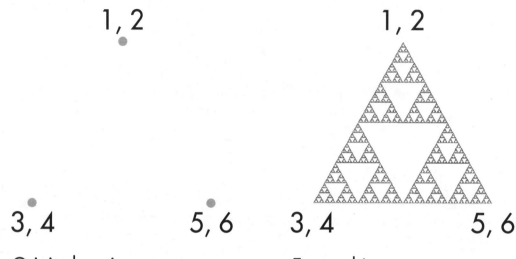

Original vertices

Eventual image

A different game: Three vertices, compression factor 2 on lower vertices, compression factor 3 on upper vertex.

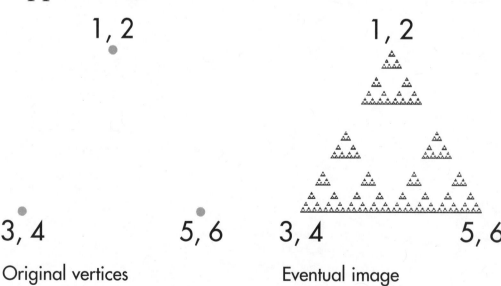

Original vertices

Eventual image

FRACTALS: A TOOL KIT OF DYNAMICS ACTIVITIES
©1999 KEY CURRICULUM PRESS

In the previous section, we saw that when you played the chaos game, the result was the Sierpiński triangle. Here we will vary the rules of the chaos game and see that different fractal images result. In fact, we will see that any fractals you generate using geometric constructions can also be generated randomly—that is, by a particular choice of rules for a chaos game.

TECHNOLOGY TIP

To get the most of this section, you should have some software available. If you have access to the World Wide Web, you may use the Java applet "Fractalina," available at **http://math.bu.edu/DYSYS/applets**. You can also play versions of the chaos game using the software Fractal Attraction, published by Academic Press.

PLAYING THE GAME WITH THREE VERTICES AND A COMPRESSION FACTOR OF 2

In our original chaos game, we need to specify three vertices. The iteration rule is: Given a seed in the triangle, choose one of the vertices randomly and move the point half the distance to the chosen vertex. As you know, the image that results from playing this game (after removing the first few iterations) is the famous fractal known as the Sierpiński triangle.

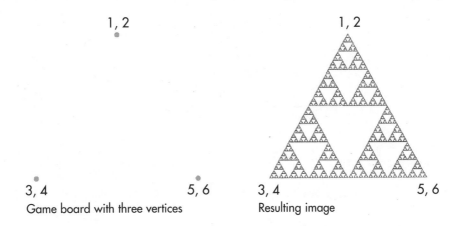

Game board with three vertices   Resulting image

Notice that you need two numbers to specify the rules of the chaos game: the number of vertices (3) and the compression factor (2). Curiously, these are exactly the numbers you encounter when you examine the self-similarity of the Sierpiński triangle. This fractal consists of three self-similar copies, and the entire image is two times the size of each copy. Is this a coincidence? Let's see.

PLAYING THE GAME WITH THREE VERTICES AND DIFFERENT COMPRESSION FACTORS

Let's change the rules of the chaos game. Suppose we use the same three vertices of an equilateral triangle as before but modify the rules by which we move our point. We'll leave the compression factor of 2 for the lower vertices, but for the upper vertex we'll use a compression factor of 3. This means that, if you roll 3 or 4, you move the point half the distance toward the lower left vertex. Similarly, if you roll 5 or 6, you move half the distance toward the lower right vertex. However, when you roll 1 or 2, your point moves two-thirds of the distance toward that vertex. That is, we move our point so that the new distance between the point and the vertex is compressed by a factor of 3.

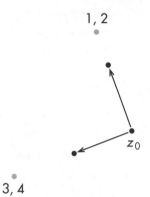

Note that in the figure above, z_0 is moved two-thirds of the distance toward vertex 1, 2, but only one-half of the distance toward 3, 4.

When we play the chaos game with these rules, we no longer find the Sierpiński triangle as the result. Rather, after eliminating the first few iterations, the result looks like the image on the right.

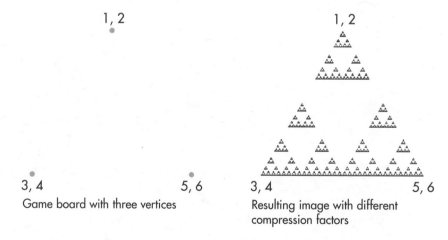

Game board with three vertices

Resulting image with different compression factors

This image contains three self-similar pieces. The lower two pieces are larger than the top piece. Indeed, it looks like the lower pieces are approximately half the size of the whole figure, but the top piece is smaller—about one-third of the size of the whole image. So our observation above holds here as well. We started with three vertices and ended up with three self-similar copies. But the two copies corresponding to the lower vertices are compressed by 2, just as the

FRACTALS: A TOOL KIT OF DYNAMICS ACTIVITIES
©1999 KEY CURRICULUM PRESS

compression rule for these vertices indicated. And the top copy is compressed by 3—again, as the rule indicated. As with the original chaos game, it appears that we can read off the rules of the chaos game from the resulting fractal.

PLAYING THE GAME WITH FIVE VERTICES AND A COMPRESSION FACTOR OF 3

You can play the chaos game with more than three vertices. Suppose we decide instead to use five vertices at the corners and center of a square. This time each vertex gets a compression factor of 3. To play this game in a manner similar to a three-vertex game, a fair die with five or ten sides would be needed, but such a die is fairly hard to find. To choose the whole numbers 1 through 5 randomly to make the moves, you can use the random number generator on a calculator or you can put five slips of paper, each marked with a different number from 1 to 5, in a jar and choose them randomly. Remember to put each number back after it's chosen and mix the numbered slips well before choosing another for the next vertex.

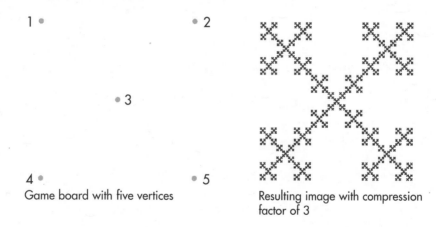

Game board with five vertices

Resulting image with compression factor of 3

This resulting image is the Fractal X. Note that it consists of five self-similar pieces (exactly the number of vertices we began with), and each copy is $\frac{1}{3}$ of the size of the original (showing our compression rule of 3). So we see again that you can determine the rules of the chaos game from the resulting fractal image.

A RANDOM MESS

You do not always get a fractal when you play the chaos game. You must place the vertices such that no overlaps occur when you contract toward a certain vertex. If you place your original vertices without care, then the image generated is a mess. For example, if you choose four vertices at the following locations and use a compression factor of 2, you get the following image.

Game board with four vertices

Resulting image with compression factor of 2

Although the resulting image does exhibit some self-similarity, it is certainly not self-similar at every one of its points.

1 ▷ SIX VERTICES AND A COMPRESSION FACTOR OF 3

TECHNOLOGY TIP

You should use the applet Fractalina at the Web site below or some other equivalent software to complete these investigations.

http://math.bu.edu/DYSYS/applets/fractalina.html

Suppose you play the chaos game with six vertices arranged at the vertices of a regular hexagon. If you are not using technology, number these vertices from 1 to 6 and use a regular die. This time, you will move two-thirds of the distance toward each vertex at each roll. That is, the original distance from the point in the orbit to the vertex will be compressed by 3.

In this picture, the point z_0 moves two-thirds of the distance to vertex 1, ending at the point z_1.

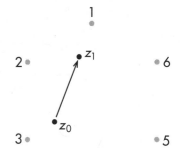

a. Given the points z_0 and z_1 on the right, continue sketching the next three points in the orbit for the hexagon if we roll 1, 5, 2, 4 in succession.

b. Now what attractor results if you play this game as before with hundreds of iterations? Before playing the game, make a guess at what you expect the resulting attractor to look like. Sketch your guess below and describe it in a few words.

c. Now play the chaos game with these rules. Sketch the resulting image to the right and describe it below. How many self-similar pieces do you see? What are their corresponding compression factors? How good was your prediction?

2 ▷ THREE VERTICES AND THREE DIFFERENT COMPRESSION FACTORS

Suppose you play the chaos game with the following rules:
Begin with three vertices of an equilateral triangle as in
the original chaos game. Compress by a factor of 2 when
the lower left vertex is chosen; by a factor of 3 when the
top vertex is chosen; and by a factor of 4 when the lower
right vertex is chosen. That is, you move $\frac{1}{2}$ of the distance
toward the lower left vertex, $\frac{2}{3}$ of the distance toward
the top vertex, and $\frac{3}{4}$ of the distance toward the lower
right vertex.

a. Before you play this game, make a guess at what you expect the resulting fractal to
look like. Sketch your guess above and describe it in a few words below.

_____

b. Now play the chaos game with these rules. Sketch the
resulting image and describe it below. How many self-
similar pieces do you see? What are their corresponding
compression factors? How good was your prediction?

_____

_____

3 ▷ FIVE VERTICES AND A COMPRESSION FACTOR OF 2.5

Suppose you play the chaos game with the five vertices of a regular pentagon.
Use a compression of 2.5, which is midway between 3 and 2.

a. What did you expect to find? What do you find?

_____

_____

b. How many self-similar copies does your attractor have? What is the
compression factor?

_____

_____

4 ▷ COMPRESSION FACTOR 2 ON THE CORNERS OF A SQUARE

Now play the chaos game with vertices at the corners of a square and a compression factor of 2.

a. What do you expect to find?

_____

b. What *do* you find?

_____

c. Are you surprised?

_____

d. The image that results from this chaos game does not appear to be a fractal, much less a Sierpiński square. But can it be divided into the correct number of self-similar copies with the right compression factor? How?

_____

_____

e. Describe a compression factor that will give you a Sierpiński square.

_____

_____

5 ▷ USING JUST TWO VERTICES

a. What do you expect would result if you played the chaos game with just two vertices (the endpoints of a line segment) and a compression factor of 2?

_____

_____

b. What if the compression factor were 3?

_____

_____

6 ▷ DESCRIBE THE GAME

For each fractal image below, describe the game that would generate the image. Make sure to include the following: the number of vertices in the game, the locations of the vertices, and the compression factor for each vertex.

a. 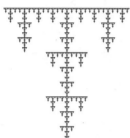   b.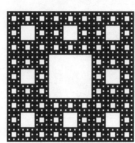

a. _____

b. _____

7 ▷ TARGET PRACTICE

a. Suppose you play the chaos game with four vertices at the corners of a square and a compression factor of 2. Sketch the orbit of the given seed on the right if the vertices are called in the following order: *A, C, D, B, B.*

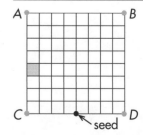

Using the same rules, describe a sequence of vertices that would bring the orbit into the interior of each shaded region below. Try to keep your sequence as short as possible.

b. _____   c. _____   d. _____

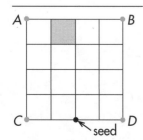   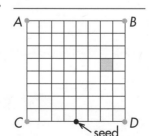   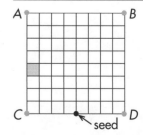

FRACTALS: A TOOL KIT OF DYNAMICS ACTIVITIES
©1999 KEY CURRICULUM PRESS

1. Below are several fractal images. Each was obtained by playing the chaos game using a certain number of vertices and a fixed compression factor. For each image, describe the game that would generate the image. Make sure to include the following in your description:

   ⬧ the number of vertices

   ⬧ the locations of the vertices

   ⬧ the (approximate) compression factor for each vertex. (*Hint:* All but one of these images has the same compression factor at each vertex. One has two different compression factors.)

   You may want to test your answers by playing the chaos game yourself.

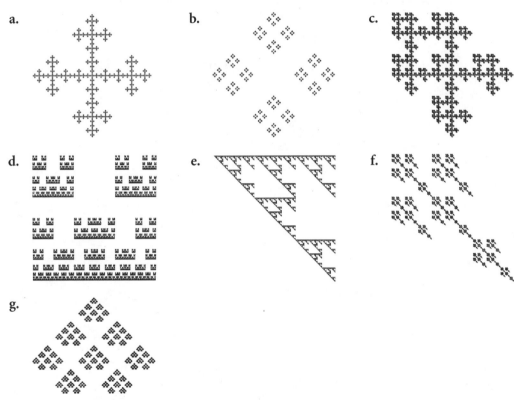

a.   b.   c.
d.   e.   f.
g.

TECHNOLOGY TIP

You can use the applet Fractalina at the Web site below or some other equivalent software to test your games.

http://math.bu.edu/DYSYS/applets/fractalina.html

2. Recall the rules of the chaos game that produced the Sierpiński hexagon. In order to write down the formulas for the six moves in this chaos game, we first need to identify the six vertices. Let's say that the origin lies right in the center of the hexagon and that the sides of the hexagon each have length 1. Since this is a regular hexagon, all of the internal angles are 120°.

At which point on the *y*-axis is vertex 1 located? (*Hint:* Draw the triangle whose vertices are located at vertex 1, vertex 2, and the origin. What can you say about the angles and the sides of this triangle?) Using this information, locate the other five vertices.

3. To write down the rules for moving a point two-thirds of the distance from one point, say (x_0, y_0), toward a vertex located at (a, b), we need to think a bit. In the picture at right the distance from *a* to x_0 must be three times as long as the distance from *a* to x_1. In terms of mathematics, we must have

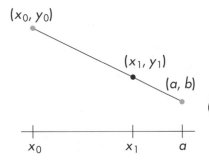

$$a - x_0 = 3(a - x_1)$$

$$3x_1 = 3a - a + x_0$$

$$x_1 = \tfrac{2}{3}a + \tfrac{1}{3}x_0$$

Similarly, the formula for y_1 is

$$y_1 = \tfrac{2}{3}b + \tfrac{1}{3}y_0$$

With this information, you should now be able to write down the formulas for moving a point two-thirds of the distance toward any of the six vertices in the previous exercise. List all of these formulas.

4. Given the results of the previous two exercises, write a program for a programmable calculator that plays the chaos game with these six vertices and a compression factor of 3.

Rotations and the Chaos Game

OVERVIEW

This lesson expands the chaos game to include rotations as well as contractions around individual vertices. This lesson will help students develop a keen geometric sense! A much more detailed analysis of the Koch curve from a mathematical perspective is offered in Further Exploration. This lesson is not intended for middle school students, although they might take a guess-and-check approach to some of the "games" in Investigations 4 and 5.

MATHEMATICAL PREREQUISITES

Students need to have a fairly good understanding of geometric transformations—in particular, dilations and rotations. A strong ability to visualize spatially is also helpful! In Further Exploration with the Koch curve, a background in coordinate geometry and systems of equations is essential along with knowledge of either the Pythagorean theorem or the 30°-60°-90° triangle relationships.

MATHEMATICAL CONNECTIONS

Topics from your mathematics curriculum that have connections to this lesson are **geometric transformations** and an introduction to **linear algebra**. The Lesson Notes below and Answers in the back describe links to more specific concepts and skills.

TECHNOLOGY

This lesson requires the use of the Web-site software to test students' hypotheses regarding the sample chaos games. There are also fractal movies available on the Web site. Students may also use the software "Franimate" on the Web site to create their own movies. (See the Technology Tip in Investigation 5.) Further Exploration activity on the Koch curve suggests that students write a computer program to generate the curve.

SUGGESTED LESSON PLAN

CLASS TIME

The activities in this lesson are fairly open-ended and exploratory in nature. Most of the work would go on in a computer lab environment. The amount of time devoted would vary greatly, depending on the interest level of the teacher and students and the course in which the work is being incorporated.

PREPARATION

You may want to make copies of the Explanation pages for students to read, or you may present the introductory material by using the Web-site software or by copying some of the graphics onto transparencies. For Investigation 1, it may be helpful to use the halfway ruler from the first investigation of Lesson 5: The Chaos Game. Also, have dice handy during Investigation 1 so students can randomly select vertices.

LESSON DEVELOPMENT

This will really depend on the skills level of the class and the amount of computer time available for accessing the Web site.

LESSON NOTES

Refer to the Explanation pages and Answers in the back.

In this section we will add a new kind of allowable rule to the chaos game. Not only will we allow contractions toward vertices, but we will also allow rotations around particular vertices. Here is an example.

A SINGLE ROTATION

Start with the three vertices of an equilateral triangle as in our original chaos game. Call the top vertex 1, 2 and the lower vertices 3, 4 and 5, 6 to correspond to the six sides of a die. Whenever one of the lower two vertices is chosen, move your point half the distance toward that vertex, just as in the original chaos game. But when the top vertex is chosen, do two things. First move your point half the distance toward that vertex. Then rotate the point around the top vertex by 90° in the counterclockwise direction. The picture above shows this new rule: We first move the point z_0 half the distance toward vertex 1, 2; then we rotate this point 90° around this vertex in the counterclockwise direction, ending at the point z_1.

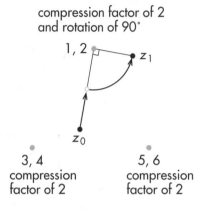

compression factor of 2 and rotation of 90°

3, 4
compression factor of 2

5, 6
compression factor of 2

If we now roll 5, we move half the distance to the vertex marked 5, 6 but do not rotate.

If we next roll 1, we again move half the distance toward 1, 2 and rotate by 90° in the counterclockwise direction.

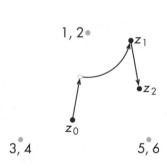

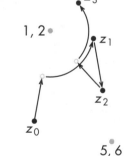

The image that results from playing the chaos game with these rules is significantly different from the images we have encountered before. This new image is pictured at the right.

READING OFF THE RULES

Look closely at this fractal image. It consists of three self-similar copies, just as we expect. But there is a difference. The two lower self-similar copies look like the entire figure, only half the size. But the top copy is different: It too is a half-sized copy of the entire figure, but is rotated 90° in the counterclockwise direction.

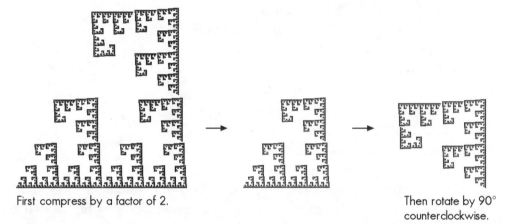

First compress by a factor of 2.   Then rotate by 90° counterclockwise.

Again we see that we can read off the rules of the chaos game by looking at the image. You may not have been able to predict what this fractal would look like before playing the chaos game, but once you see it, you can figure out the rules that generated it!

A DIFFERENT ROTATION

Now suppose we change the rules. This time, instead of rotating 90° around the top vertex, we'll rotate 180°. (The rules at the other vertices remain unchanged.) If we play the chaos game with these rules, a different fractal appears. Maybe you could not predict what the fractal would look like before you played the game, but if you look closely at the image on the right, you'll recognize the rules.

Again we see three self-similar pieces. The entire fractal has its wider part at the bottom and a narrower part at the top. That's true of the two lower pieces as well. But the top piece is different: Its narrow part is at the bottom, and the wide part is at the top. This piece has been rotated by 180°, just as the rules suggest.

TECHNOLOGY TIP

To test the following versions of the chaos game, use the Web page at:

http://math.bu.edu/DYSYS/applets/fractalina.html

1 ▹ THE TOP VERTEX WITH A TWIST

Suppose you play the chaos game using the three vertices of an equilateral triangle. Call the top vertex 1, 2 and the two lower vertices 3, 4 and 5, 6. As usual, you roll a die and move toward the vertex corresponding to the number that appears. The rules for these moves are as follows:

▵ When you roll 3 or 4, move the point half the distance to the lower left vertex.

▵ When you roll 5 or 6, move the point half the distance toward the lower right vertex.

▵ When you roll 1 or 2, first move half the distance toward the top vertex, then rotate by 90° in the *clockwise* direction.

In the following three problems sketch the orbit of the given seed z_0 for the given rolls of the die.

a. You roll 1, 5, 6.   **b.** You roll 1, 2, 3.   **c.** You roll 1, 2, 1, 2.

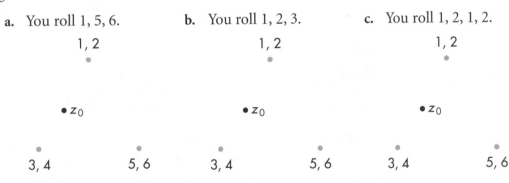

d. Which of the following three fractals will result if we play this chaos game for a long time?

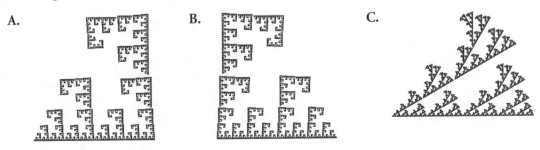

A.   B.   C.

e. Look at the two fractals that you did not choose as the answer to the last question. How do you think each one was generated? Describe the compression factor and rotation for each vertex. (*Hint:* All three were generated with the same vertices.)

_____

_____

_____

2 ▹ BOTTOM VERTICES GET A TWIST

Here are the rules for a different chaos game:

A
• Move half the distance to *A* when *A* is selected.

B
When *B* is selected, first move half the distance to *B*, then rotate 45¡ clockwise.

C
When *C* is selected, first move half the distance to *C*, then rotate 45¡ counterclockwise.

a. Which of the following three fractals is generated by this chaos game? (The fractals are not drawn to scale.) Try to determine this first by playing the game by hand above. Then play the game using technology to check your guess.

A.

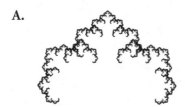

B.

C.

b. Look at the two fractals that you did not choose as the answer to the last question. How do you think each one was generated? Describe the compression factor and the rotation for each vertex. (*Hint:* All three were generated with the same vertices.)

_____

_____

_____

3 ▹ THE KOCH CURVE

The Koch curve shown below is one of the more famous fractals. Can the Koch curve be generated by playing the chaos game? Let's see. To begin, this fractal consists of four self-similar pieces, each of which has a contraction factor of $1/3$. But these pieces are not all in a line. Some seem to be rotated:

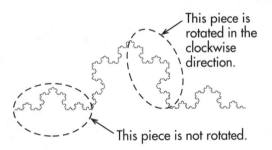

This piece is rotated in the clockwise direction.

This piece is not rotated.

So we would expect to obtain the Koch curve by playing the chaos game with four vertices, a contraction factor of $1/3$, and a couple of rotations. Try to find experimentally the locations of the four vertices and the appropriate rotations that will generate the Koch curve. Describe your results here.

_____

_____

_____

4 ▷ DESCRIBE THE GAME

Here are a few fractals generated by chaos games that involve various rotations. Identify the chaos game someone would need to play in order to generate each. You should indicate the number of vertices, their locations, the compression factors, and the rotations at each vertex. If possible, test out your answers by playing the chaos game you describe in each case.

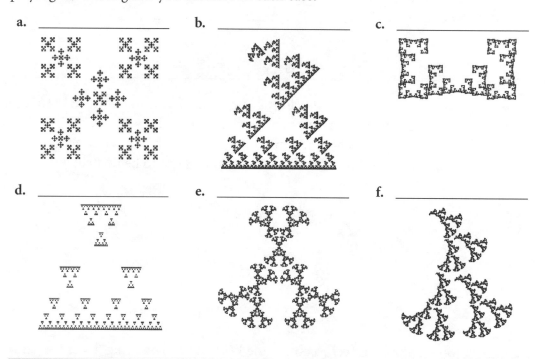

a. _____ b. _____ c. _____

d. _____ e. _____ f. _____

5 ▷ MOVIES

Now that you can use rotations in the chaos game, you can make movies of these fractals changing over time by just changing the rotations a little bit in each frame of the film. That is what you see on the next page. Since a book is not the best place to view movies, we can only show you selected frames from the movie. You can see the actual movie if you visit our Web site:

http://math.bu.edu/DYSYS/movies.html

Select the Dancing Sierpiński Movie.

Here are selected frames from the film.

a. Your job is to figure out how we made this film. Each frame is an attractor for a particular chaos game. How did we make each frame? That is, how many vertices were involved, what was the compression factor, and what, if any, rotations were involved? Finally, how did we create the "motion"? That is, what have we changed as we progress from frame to frame?

_____

_____

_____

By the way, if you would like to make your own "fractal film," check out the movie-making applet "Franimate" at **http://math.bu.edu/DYSYS/applets**.

1. These problems are quite challenging! Here are a few fractals generated by chaos games that involve various rotations. Identify the chaos game someone would need to play in order to generate each. You should indicate the number of vertices, their locations, and the compression factor and rotation at each vertex. If possible, test your answer by playing the chaos game you describe in each case.

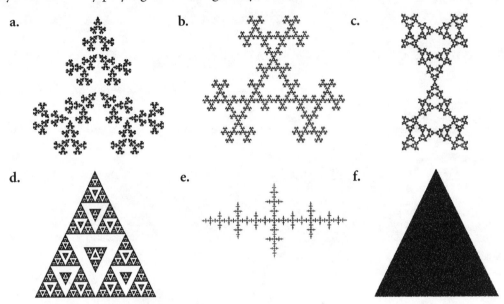

a.   b.   c.

d.   e.   f.

These are not so easy!!!

2. **Formulas for the Koch curve.** You can determine the exact locations of the vertices that produce the Koch curve using the chaos game. Or, equivalently, you can write down explicit formulas for the transformations that produce these smaller self-similar copies. Here's how. First, suppose the generator is the unit interval $0 \leq x \leq 1$. This interval clearly defines two vertices in the coordinate plane: the origin and the point $(1, 0)$. When we play the chaos game and these vertices are chosen, the rule is: Move $2/3$ of the distance toward whichever vertex is chosen. We can see this by simply contracting the Koch curve by $1/3$ toward either end, as shown here:

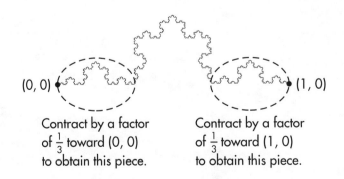

$(0, 0)$ $(1, 0)$

Contract by a factor
of $\frac{1}{3}$ toward $(0, 0)$
to obtain this piece.

Contract by a factor
of $\frac{1}{3}$ toward $(1, 0)$
to obtain this piece.

a. What are the transformations that produce these two contractions? Let's try to write down their explicit formulas in terms of (x_0, y_0).

So the question is: What are the other two vertices? These are tougher to find. Applying the Pythagorean theorem, we get these segment lengths:

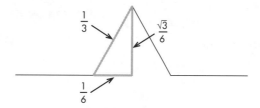

So we have the following coordinates on the generator:

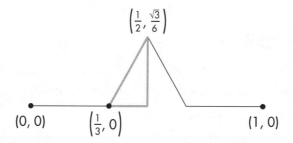

Let's work with the transformation that takes the original segment (connecting $(0, 0)$ and $(1, 0)$) and shrinks it and places it down on the segment connecting $(\frac{1}{3}, 0)$ and $(\frac{1}{2}, \sqrt{3}/6)$. In particular, the transformation takes $(0, 0)$ to $(\frac{1}{3}, 0)$ and $(1, 0)$ to $(\frac{1}{2}, \sqrt{3}/6)$. We can use this information to determine the exact formula for this transformation.

The major idea here is that this transformation is **linear**. That means that the transformation assumes the very special form:

$$x_1 = Ax_0 + By_0 + C$$

$$y_1 = Dx_0 + Ey_0 + F$$

So if we determine the values of the constants A–F we have our formula.

Luckily, we have some information about this transformation. We know that the point $(0, 0)$ is taken to $(1/3, 0)$ by this transformation. So if we substitute $(0, 0)$ for (x_0, y_0), then we know that (x_1, y_1) must be given by $(1/3, 0)$. Making these replacements in the above equations yields:

$$\frac{1}{3} = A \cdot 0 + B \cdot 0 + C$$

$$0 = D \cdot 0 + E \cdot 0 + F$$

So we see that C must be $1/3$ and F must be 0. We also know that $(1, 0)$ is taken to $(1/2, \sqrt{3}/6)$. So if we substitute $(1, 0)$ for (x_0, y_0), then we know that (x_1, y_1) must be given by $(1/2, \sqrt{3}/6)$. That is, we know:

$$\frac{1}{2} = A \cdot 1 + B \cdot 0 + \frac{1}{3}$$

$$\frac{\sqrt{3}}{6} = D \cdot 1 + E \cdot 0 + 0$$

Solving these equations yields $A = 1/6$ and $D = \sqrt{3}/6$.

b. So now we know the constants A, C, D, and F. We must only figure out B and E. This is a fairly difficult exercise using similar triangles. Go ahead and find B and E.

c. Now we have all of the coefficients in our transformation. Recall that what we are interested in finding are the points to which we are contracting toward and then rotating around. To find these points, we must find the fixed point for this transformation. That is, we need to find the point (x_0, y_0) that satisfies:

$$x_0 = Ax_0 + By_0 + C$$

$$y_0 = Dx_0 + Ey_0 + F$$

It looks like there are lots of letters here, but actually we have already determined A–F. So all we need to do is substitute these values and then solve for x_0 and y_0. Go for it!

In a similar fashion, you can find the coordinates of the transformation that produces the other rotated portion of the Koch curve.

d. Once you have written down all of these transformations, write a program to generate the Koch curve.

Investigating Sierpiński

OVERVIEW

The lesson is a collection of investigations, many of which could be done independently of one another and with little previous experience with fractals. The lesson does not contain an Explanation section, for all new material is made clear within each investigation. Also, there are no Further Exploration problems. This lesson focuses on the Sierpiński triangle, the Sierpiński tetrahedron, and the Sierpiński hexagon and investigates a variety of ways to generate these fractals. Other investigations give suggestions for constructing models of the triangle and tetrahedron.

MATHEMATICAL CONNECTIONS

Students need to be familiar with the Sierpiński triangle itself, with geometric shapes such as triangles, hexagons, and tetrahedra, and with a method for computing the area of a hexagon.

MATHEMATICAL PREREQUISITES

Topics from your mathematics curriculum that have connections to different parts of this lesson are **Pascal's triangle**, **recognizing patterns**, **three-dimensional geometry**, **volume**, and **computer science**. Links to more specific concepts and skills are included in the Lesson Notes below and in teacher annotations to the solutions.

TECHNOLOGY

A computer drawing program could come in handy for Investigation 8. You might also want to use graphing calculators to graph the "growth" of perimeters, volume, number of self-similar objects, and so on.

SUGGESTED LESSON PLAN

CLASS TIME

Most of these investigations would probably be done outside of class, as individual or group projects. Portions of a 50-minute class period might be set aside for groups to meet. If the class as a whole takes on the construction of a giant Sierpiński tetrahedron, several 50-minute class periods might need to be devoted to the actual assembly process after subassemblies are done outside of class. Also, keep in mind that many of these investigations can stand alone, and all of them make excellent projects.

PREPARATION

Make sure that "building" supplies are available for the selected investigations. See each investigation for the necessary supplies.

LESSON DEVELOPMENT

This depends entirely on which investigations you choose to have students do.

LESSON NOTES

In Investigation 6, the constructions using toothpicks and marshmallows will have size limitations due to weight and structural strength. Many classrooms around the country have tackled the construction of a giant Sierpiński tetrahedron, where each of the smallest tetrahedra were made from sturdy paper such as card stock. Some of the first school groups to do this found that within 24 hours after completion, sections of the tetrahedron would sag or collapse under the weight; schools that have attempted this more recently are reinforcing the frames with metal rods. Another inexpensive method for making a fairly strong tetrahedron involves cutting and folding a $3\frac{5}{8}'' \times 6\frac{1}{2}''$ envelope. Seal the envelope, and fold along both diagonals. Unfold and cut out one of the obtuse isosceles triangles indicated by the folds and a long edge. Then open the envelope up into a "boat" and insert one pointed end of the boat all the way inside the other.

1 ▹ THE WORLD'S LARGEST SIERPIŃSKI TRIANGLE!

So far, we have always drawn the Sierpiński triangle by starting with a fixed triangle and "working inward." That is, we start with a fixed triangle and begin removing smaller copies of the triangle. This way the resulting image always has a fixed size. But we can also generate an object like the Sierpiński triangle by "working outward." Here's the way to do this. Everyone in class should start with the same large equilateral triangle on a sheet of paper. Use the image below, or a photocopy of it.

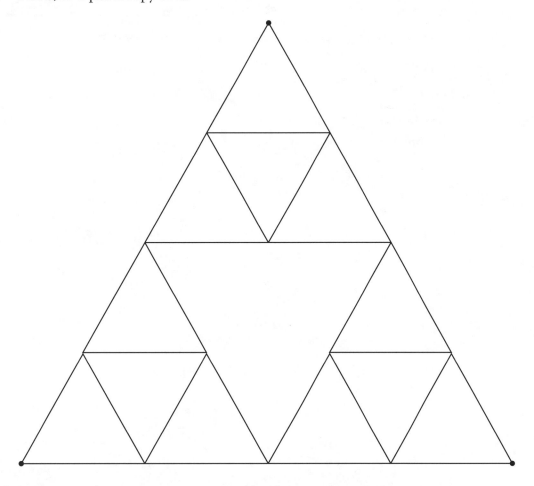

You'll first work inward before you work outward. Using a pen and a ruler, draw the outline of the Sierpiński triangle down to a certain stage on your own sheet of paper. Make sure that the smaller triangles are placed in exactly the right positions. Above is a drawing that is complete to stage 2; you should go at least to stage 4.

Now assemble all of the triangles by matching their vertices. If there are only nine people in your class, you will not get a very large Sierpiński triangle. If there are 27 people in your class, the end result of your labors will be larger. If you can recruit your family and friends to create a few more Sierpiński triangles, you could eventually create the world's largest Sierpiński triangle!

For example, if each original triangle has sides of length 10 centimeters, you need only three copies to produce a larger triangle whose base is 20 centimeters long.

a. How many copies would you need to produce a Sierpiński triangle whose base is 40 centimeters long? _____

b. How about 80 centimeters long? (That's almost one meter.) _____

c. How about 160 centimeters? _____

d. How about 100 meters (or so)? _____

That's one large Sierpiński triangle! You'd better start recruiting your friends and family!

2 ▷ PASCAL'S TRIANGLE

Pascal's triangle is another famous triangle in mathematics. You might think there is no connection between the Pascal triangle and the Sierpiński triangle, since one arises in algebra and the other comes from geometry. But wait a minute—let's look a little more closely at Pascal's triangle.

```
      1
     1 1
    1 2 1
   1 3 3 1
  1 4 6 4 1
 1 5 10 10 5 1
_ _ _ _ _ _ _
_ _ _ _ _ _ _ _
```

Study the numbers above until you figure out how to generate Pascal's triangle. Then fill in the next two rows.

Now, instead of using the whole numbers in Pascal's triangle, let's change the triangle so that it records only if the entry is even or odd. Start with a triangle filled with circles, as shown at the right. Shade a circle whenever the corresponding entry in Pascal's triangle is odd, and leave the circle unshaded whenever the entry is even. We have filled in the first three rows to get you started.

a. Do you notice something interesting as you fill in this diagram? Explain.

_____

_____

b. Explain a procedure for deciding whether to shade a circle based on the shading of the circles directly above it.

_____

_____

c. Explain how the procedure you just described is related to the addition of odd and even numbers.

_____

_____

3 ▷ SHADING DIFFERENT CIRCLES

Let's try a slightly different rule for shading the circles. Previously, you shaded the circle whenever the corresponding entry was odd and left the circle unshaded when the entry was even. Another way to say this is that you shaded the circle if the entry was not exactly divisible by 2 and left it unshaded if the entry was divisible by 2. Let's modify the rule and divide instead by 3. That is, shade a circle if the corresponding entry in Pascal's triangle is not divisible by 3, and leave the circle unshaded if it is divisible by 3. Now what pattern emerges? Fill in the following diagram using this rule. We have started you off by filling in the first four rows.

Describe your results here. What pattern now emerges? Is this the same as the previous case? Have you seen this fractal before? How was it generated?

_____

_____

_____

4 ▷ CELLULAR AUTOMATA

You can construct large, fractal-like images using a process called **cellular automata**. A cellular automaton is an iteration rule that converts strings of 0's and 1's into other strings of 0's and 1's. *(Automata* is the plural of *automaton.)* These types of rules are of tremendous importance in computer science, where it is common to encode information in strings of 0's and 1's. Rather than use 0's and 1's, you will use shaded and unshaded circles so you can more clearly see the geometric pattern that emerges.

TECHNOLOGY TIP

A famous example of a cellular automaton is "The Game of Life." This game, invented by the mathematician John Conway, uses circles on a rectangular grid. You can play this game on paper, but it works more efficiently on a computer.

Here is a simple example of a cellular automaton. We begin with a seed that is an infinite string of unshaded and shaded circles. For example, our seed may be all unshaded circles:

or a single shaded circle flanked by all unshaded ones:

or whatever:

To describe the rule, we start with a seed and then place a blank row of circles below it so that each of the lower circles is wedged directly between two upper circles:

The pair of circles above each circle in the second row determines the shading of that circle. If the two circles above are both shaded or both unshaded, then the lower circle is left unshaded. But if one of the two upper circles is shaded and the other unshaded, then the lower circle is shaded.

We can summarize these rules as follows:

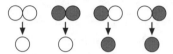

That is, the second row for the above seed should be

since two adjacent unshaded circles yield an unshaded circle below, and the two pairs of adjacent circles that include one unshaded and one shaded circle each yield a shaded circle below.

A different seed yields a different pattern:

a. Now begin with the following seed and iterate by the above rule, using each successive row to generate the row beneath it.

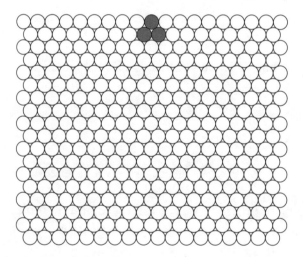

b. What pattern eventually emerges?

_____

_____

_____

FRACTALS: A TOOL KIT OF DYNAMICS ACTIVITIES
©1999 KEY CURRICULUM PRESS

5 ▷ FRACTALS IN 3-D—THE SIERPIŃSKI TETRAHEDRON

If you can build a Sierpiński triangle, you should also be able to build a Sierpiński tetrahedron. The easiest way to do this is to use the "copies of copies" approach. Start with a tetrahedron (recall that this is a three-dimensional solid figure with four triangular faces). In a regular tetrahedron, each of the four faces is an equilateral triangle. Now find a copy machine that makes three-dimensional copies. If you cannot find such a machine, you'll just have to imagine the process. Or, you can jump ahead to the next investigation and start building your own Sierpiński tetrahedron out of toothpicks.

Start with a tetrahedron. Call this stage 0 of the process.

Then compress it by a factor of 2 and make four (not three) copies. Reassemble the smaller copies so that they fit exactly into the shell of the original tetrahedron.

a. Imagine repeating the "copies of copies" process, and fill in the following table.

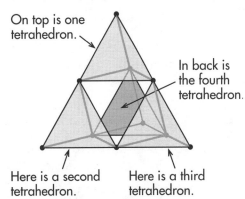

On top is one tetrahedron.

In back is the fourth tetrahedron.

Here is a second tetrahedron.

Here is a third tetrahedron.

Stage number	0	1	2	3	4	n
Number of tetrahedra	1					
Volume of each tetrahedron (cubic units)	1					
Total volume (cubic units)	1					

6 ▷ BUILD YOUR OWN SIERPIŃSKI TETRAHEDRON

One way to build a Sierpiński tetrahedron is to use a lot of toothpicks and tiny marshmallows. With the marshmallows at the vertices and the toothpicks forming the edges, you can assemble a single small tetrahedron like the one in this picture.

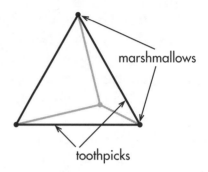

marshmallows

toothpicks

Stale marshmallows are better for construction purposes because the resulting structure does not bend as much. (Also, you tend not to eat as many if they are stale.)

You can now build the world's largest Sierpiński tetrahedron. Simply have all of your classmates and friends assemble small tetrahedra, and then gather their work to put it all together.

In order to estimate your toothpick and marshmallow requirements, let's first estimate how much of each ingredient your Sierpiński tetrahedron will need.

a. How many toothpicks will you need for each small tetrahedron? _____

b. How many marshmallows? _____

Now, it would seem that, at the next stage of construction (that is, stage 1), we would need four times as many marshmallows and toothpicks. After all, you put four small pieces together to make the larger piece. But this piece will not be assembled by simply joining together four small tetrahedra. This is because several of the junction points will already have marshmallows in place. For example, when you join the first two tetrahedra together, you will have one extra marshmallow (which you can eat).

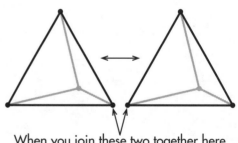

When you join these two together here, you have an extra marshmallow

c. When you attach the third small tetrahedron to form the base of the larger figure, how many extra marshmallows will you have? _____

d. And when you add the "top" tetrahedron, how many more extra marshmallows will you have? _____

   e. How many extra marshmallows do you have so far? (Make sure you count them before you eat them.) _____

   f. So how many total marshmallows do you need at stage 1 of the construction? _____

   g. And how many toothpicks do you need? _____

   h. At stage 2 you need: _____ marshmallows _____ toothpicks

   i. At stage 3: _____ marshmallows _____ toothpicks

   j. At stage 4: _____ marshmallows _____ toothpicks

   k. At stage n: _____ marshmallows _____ toothpicks

   l. How many extra marshmallows do you have at stage n? _____

   m. How many of these will you have eaten? _____

   n. Suppose that the base of each individual tetrahedron is 10 centimeters. How long will each side of the base be at stage n? _____

7 ▷ UNDERSTANDING THE SIERPIŃSKI TETRAHEDRON

Now let's try to imagine what the Sierpiński tetrahedron looks like when we have iterated this process infinitely often. Consider each face. After the first iteration, what does each face look like?

   a. Draw a picture of one of the faces.

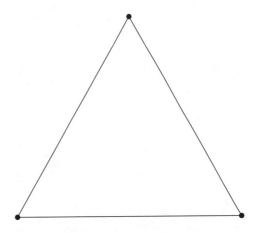

   b. What about the bottom face: Does it look the same? _____

c. After the second iteration, what does each face look like? Draw it.

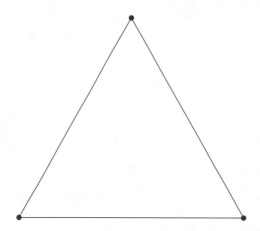

d. After iterating infinitely often, what will each face look like?

_____

_____

e. Recall that when we constructed the Sierpiński triangle by removals, we removed a middle triangle from each remaining triangle at each stage. What are we doing in the case of the tetrahedron? What is the shape of the solid region that we remove from the original tetrahedron at the first stage of the construction? Is it a tetrahedron? How many faces does the removed solid region have? Describe this solid as best you can by imagining it. You probably will want to build your own Sierpiński tetrahedron so you can see this interior space for yourself.

_____

_____

NAME(S): _____

8 ▷ THE SIERPIŃSKI HEXAGON

So far we have not spent much time discussing the Sierpiński hexagon, but this is a fascinating object as well. You will assemble this fractal using the "copies of copies" technique. To make the numbers easier to work with, fit the Sierpiński hexagon into a regular hexagon whose sides all have length 1.

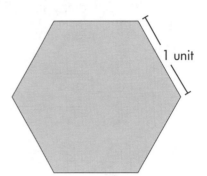

1 unit

To help answer the next few questions, first divide the hexagon above into six congruent equilateral triangles. Every triangle should have the center as one of its vertices.

  a. What are the measures of the interior angles of this hexagon? _____

  b. What is the height of the hexagon? _____

  c. What is the total area of the hexagon? _____

TECHNOLOGY TIP

Most computer drawing applications allow you to duplicate an object and also to shrink an object. To shrink several objects at once, you may need to group them first.

  d. To construct the Sierpiński hexagon, the iteration rule is: Shrink the original hexagon and then reassemble as shown here. By what compression factor should you shrink the hexagon, in order to obtain this result? _____

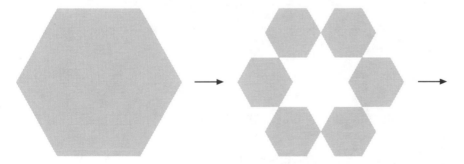

  e. What is the length of a side of any of the six smaller hexagons? _____

  f. What is the area of each of the six smaller hexagons? _____

  g. Note the star in the middle of the figure. Where have you seen that before?

_____

h. Now iterate. Sketch at least part of the next figure in this orbit.

i. How many small hexagons exist at this stage? _____

j. What does the central removed region look like?

_____

_____

k. Here is the Sierpiński hexagon after many, many iterations. You might recognize something familiar in the middle of this picture. If you do, describe it here.

_____

_____

_____

Fractal Dimension

OVERVIEW

This lesson is an extensive discussion of dimension. The discussion includes the topics of dimension in standard Euclidean geometry, topological dimension, and fractal dimension. An important part of the lesson is the material describing applications, which appears at the end of the Explanation pages. Many people feel that fractals are just a collection of pretty pictures. It is important that students realize instead that even this fairly new area of mathematics already has important applications in our lives and in the world around us and that new uses of fractal geometry continue to develop.

MATHEMATICAL PREREQUISITES

Students need to be familiar with exponents, with logarithms and their properties, and with the traditional concept of dimension. Students should also be somewhat familiar with fractals prior to working with this unit. This way they are already acquainted with what fractals look like and how varied they can be in appearance and complexity.

MATHEMATICAL CONNECTIONS

Topics from your mathematics curriculum that have connections to this lesson are **dimension**, **Euclidean** and **non-Euclidean geometry**, and **logarithms**. The applications presented also demonstrate connections to the science curriculum. The Lesson Notes below and Answers in the back describe links to more specific concepts and skills.

TECHNOLOGY

Students need calculators to evaluate logarithms when computing fractal dimensions.

SUGGESTED LESSON PLAN

CLASS TIME

One 50-minute class period to develop the concept of fractal dimension and the method for determining the dimension of a given fractal. Another 50-minute class period for more Investigations and Further Exploration problems.

PREPARATION

If students have not yet studied logarithms, they will need to learn some of the basic concepts and properties before they could work with the material in this lesson.

LESSON DEVELOPMENT

- Discuss what the concept of fractal dimension might mean in terms of indicating the degree of "roughness" or "complexity."

- There are several visual examples in the Explanation pages, but one other way to help students gain a "feel" for what fractal dimension describes is to take a piece of aluminum foil and hold it flat—a two-dimensional object. Then crumple it a little bit; it is no longer a two-dimensional flat plane, but neither does it fill space, so it is not three-dimensional. Crumple it more; now it is "rougher" or more "complex," so it has a higher dimension. The more you crumple it and start to form a solid object, the closer you appear to get to dimension 3.

- Assign a selection of problems from the Investigations and Further Exploration. The detailed explanations in the Answers sections can be helpful in deciding which problems to use in your classroom.

LESSON NOTES

You may need to remind students that when we speak of dividing a square into four pieces, each of which is $\frac{1}{2}$ of the original, we are referring to $\frac{1}{2}$ of the linear measures, not $\frac{1}{2}$ of the area.

The notes on dimensions are organized on a single page and make this page especially useful to photocopy and distribute to students.

As you probably have already seen, fractals such as the Sierpiński triangle and the Koch curve are self-similar objects. This is because if you magnify portions of these figures, you find an exact replica of the original image. But there is more to the fractal story. Besides self-similarity, most fractals enjoy another property: They usually have "fractional" dimension. This means their dimension is not a whole number, but instead is a fraction. What this refers to is a new type of dimension called *fractal dimension*.

Obviously, fractal dimension is not the usual kind of dimension. Roughly speaking, fractal dimension is a measure of the thickness or roughness of the fractal. Before discussing this notion in detail, notice that fractals with very similar generators can differ widely in appearance. For example, consider the three generators shown below.

A.   **B.**   **C.**

When we follow similar iteration rules determined by these different generators, we create the following fractals:

In each case, assume the width of the original generator is 1. The only difference between these generators is the length of each small segment. In case A, each segment of the generator has length $2/7$; in case B (the Koch curve), the length is $1/3$; and in case C, the length is $2/5$.

Even though the generators are very similar, the resulting images are very different. Fractal C is rougher and denser than fractal B, which in turn is rougher and denser than fractal A. Similarly, fractal C seems thicker than the other two, even though we used exactly the same number of iterations to produce all three images. So the fractal dimension of C should be larger than that of B, and the dimension of B should be larger than that of A. Fractal dimension gives us an exact means of measuring these numbers.

At this point you might want to look ahead to the eight fractals in Investigation 2. These eight fractals give you a chance to test your intuition for fractal dimension. Try to number the eight fractals according to relative order of thickness and roughness, using only your eye as guide. When you get to Investigation 2, you will compute the fractal dimension of each and see how accurate your estimates have been. (Just to be tricky, we have included two fractals that have the same fractal dimension.)

WHAT IS DIMENSION ANYWAY?

Before explaining what fractal dimension means, we need to take a brief detour to understand exactly what we mean by *dimension*. Now, we know intuitively that a line segment is one-dimensional, a square is two-dimensional, and a cube is three-dimensional. But why is this?

One possible explanation is that there is only one "direction" to move in a line segment (back and forth), two directions in a square region (left/right and up/down), and three in the interior space of a cube. This reasoning is a little fishy, because there are actually infinitely many possible directions to move in a square region (any point of the compass, for example). Intuitively, however, there are only two basic directions (mathematicians say there are exactly two *independent* directions).

While this concept is intuitively correct for the line segment, the square, and the cube, it does not work well for the Sierpiński triangle. In this figure we can move in more than one direction at any point, but we cannot move in every direction.

From the indicated point we can move in these initial directions.

We can change direction after the initial takeoff. For example, we could travel on this path:

But we cannot move in an arbitrary direction without leaving the fractal. For example:

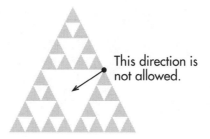

This direction is not allowed.

We have more freedom of direction here than with the line segment but less freedom than with the square, so intuitively we expect the dimension of the Sierpiński triangle to be somewhere between 1 and 2.

To understand the notion of dimension more fully, let's reexamine the line segment, square, and cube.

ONE DIMENSION: THE LINE SEGMENT

A line segment is a self-similar object. We can break a line segment into self-similar pieces.

The original is four times longer than any of the four pieces.

The original is seven times longer than any of the seven pieces.

In general, we can break the line segment into n self-similar pieces:

number of pieces = magnification factor

TWO DIMENSIONS: THE INTERIOR OF A SQUARE

The interior of a square is also a self-similar object. We can break it into smaller self-similar objects.

The original has sides two times longer than any of the four pieces.
$$4 = 2^2$$

The original has sides three times longer than any of the nine pieces.
$$9 = 3^2$$

In general, the original has sides m times longer than any of the m^2 pieces:

number of pieces = (magnification factor)^2

THREE DIMENSIONS: THE INTERIOR OF A CUBE

Finally, the interior of a cube is also self-similar. It can be decomposed into smaller cubes.

The original has sides two times longer than any of the eight cubes.
$$8 = 2^3$$

The original has sides three times longer than any of the 27 cubes.
$$27 = 3^3$$

In general, the original cube has sides m times longer than any of the m^3 pieces:

number of pieces = (magnification factor)^3

So if m is the magnification factor, a line segment may be broken into m^1 self-similar pieces; a square interior into m^2 pieces; and a cube interior into m^3 pieces. The exponent of m in each case shows the dimension of that object. This suggests the formula for the fractal dimension of an object:

$$n = m^d$$

where n = number of self-similar pieces
      m = magnification factor
      d = dimension

FRACTALS: A TOOL KIT OF DYNAMICS ACTIVITIES

BACK TO THE SIERPIŃSKI TRIANGLE

Now, what about the Sierpiński triangle? As we know, this figure may be broken into three pieces ($n = 3$), each of which may be magnified by a factor of 2 ($m = 2$) to yield the entire triangle.

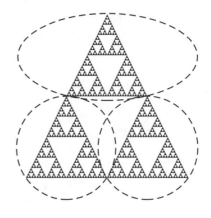

So what is the dimension of this figure?

Using $n = m^d$, we have $3 = 2^d$.

Taking the log of both sides yields:

$$\log 3 = \log\left(2^d\right)$$

Using a property of logarithms:

$$\log 3 = d \log 2$$

and hence

$$d = \frac{\log 3}{\log 2} \approx 1.585$$

So the dimension of the Sierpiński triangle is approximately 1.585.

The 3 in the expression above comes from the number of self-similar copies in the fractal, and 2 is the magnification factor. So we have discovered the formula for fractal dimension:

$$\text{dimension} = \frac{\log(\text{number of pieces})}{\log(\text{magnification factor})} \quad \text{or} \quad d = \frac{\log n}{\log m}$$

Let's check this. The Sierpiński triangle also consists of nine self-similar pieces, each with magnification factor 4. So the dimension is:

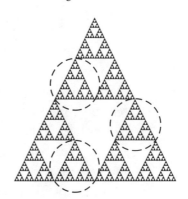

$$d = \frac{\log 9}{\log 4} = \frac{\log 3^2}{\log 2^2} = \frac{2\log 3}{2\log 2} = \frac{\log 3}{\log 2}$$

yielding the same result as before.

This dimension value, called the **fractal dimension** of the object, is not an integer in this case. For the Sierpiński triangle it is somewhere between 1 and 2, just as our intuition suggested earlier.

THE KOCH CURVE

What is the fractal dimension of the Koch curve?

As we saw earlier, this figure consists of four self-similar pieces, each with magnification factor 3. So the fractal dimension is:

$$d = \frac{\log 4}{\log 3} \approx 1.262$$

We can also break the Koch curve into 16 pieces with magnification factor 9, so the fractal dimension is:

$$d = \frac{\log 16}{\log 9} = \frac{\log 4^2}{\log 3^2} = \frac{2\log 4}{2\log 3} = \frac{\log 4}{\log 3}$$

as before. So the fractal dimension of the Koch curve is approximately 1.26, which is somewhat smaller than 1.58, the dimension of the Sierpiński triangle. This is just as we expect, as the Koch curve appears to be less "thick" than the Sierpiński triangle.

THE SIERPIŃSKI TETRAHEDRON

Earlier we looked at the fractal known as the Sierpiński tetrahedron. We saw that this fractal consisted of four self-similar pieces, each of which had magnification factor 2. Therefore the fractal dimension of this object is:

$$d = \frac{\log 4}{\log 2} = \frac{\log 2^2}{\log 2} = \frac{2\log 2}{\log 2} = 2$$

Oops, this dimension shouldn't be a whole number! Certainly the Sierpiński tetrahedron is a fractal object, so why does its dimension turn out to be 2? The answer is that a fractal must have fractal dimension that exceeds the "usual" dimension of the object. The "usual" dimension of an object is what mathematicians call **topological dimension**. This is actually a common mistake. Many people think that fractals *must* have fractional dimension, but this is not the case.

If you are wondering what the "usual" dimension of the Sierpiński tetrahedron might be, keep reading.

TOPOLOGICAL DIMENSION

Here is a rough idea of topological dimension. An object in the plane is said to have dimension 0 if you can always surround any of its set of points with arbitrarily small circles (without interior) that do not intersect the set. An object in three-dimensional space has dimension 0 if you can always surround any of its points with arbitrarily small (hollow) spheres that do not intersect the set. For example, a scattering of points in the plane or in space has topological dimension 0. But a curve in the plane does not, because you cannot find tiny circles around points on the curve that miss the curve completely.

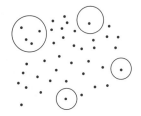

The set above is a collection of points. It has dimension 0 because we can always draw tiny circles around points and never intersect other points.

A set in the plane has dimension 1 if any of its points can be surrounded by arbitrarily small circles that intersect the set in a set of dimension 0, that is, in a set which is like a scatter of points. For example, curves in the plane have dimension 1.

The set on the right is a curve. It does not have dimension 0 because small circles around points in the set always intersect other points in the set.

Similarly, the Koch curve and the Sierpiński triangle have topological dimension 1. In particular, we can always thread small circles through the vertices of the Sierpiński triangle so that these circles intersect the set in a set of points, as shown here.

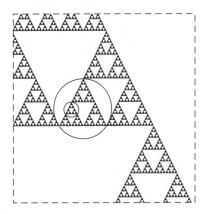

In similar fashion, we can find small spheres that meet the Sierpiński tetrahedron in only finitely many points, so the Sierpiński tetrahedron also has topological dimension 1. Since its fractal dimension is 2, this set meets the requirement that its fractal dimension exceeds its topological dimension. That's why this object is a fractal.

APPLICATIONS

Why is the notion of dimension important? In recent years, scientists and mathematicians have used the notion of fractal dimension in many different ways. For example, in medicine a cancerous tumor may be either malignant or benign. Generally, in an X-ray image, a malignant tumor appears to be a complicated shape with many tendrils, while a benign tumor is often encapsulated or smoother. How do radiologists differentiate between the two? One measure of the roughness of the tumor is the fractal dimension of its X-ray image. The smaller the dimension, the better the chance that the tumor is benign.

In addition, geologists measure the fractal dimension of the fractures in the earth's surface to predict when and where earthquakes will appear. Ecologists compute fractal dimensions of forests to gauge the health of the ecosystem. Art historians use fractal dimension to estimate the age of certain ancient Asian paintings. And computer scientists use fractals to help compress large sets of data for efficient transmission via satellite.

1 ▷ FAMOUS FRACTALS

Sketch a rough image of each fractal in the space provided. Then determine for each:

▲ A number of self-similar pieces that you could divide the fractal into.

▲ The magnification factor that goes with the number of self-similar pieces you chose.

▲ The fractal dimension of the fractal.

a. The Sierpiński triangle

_____

_____

_____

_____

b. The Cantor middle-thirds set

_____

_____

_____

_____

c. The Koch curve

_____

_____

_____

_____

d. The Sierpiński tetrahedron

_____

_____

_____

_____

2 ▷ ORDERING FRACTALS BY DIMENSION

⊿ Look at the fractals that follow and try to number them according to their relative dimension. Number the fractal you think has the highest dimension "8," and the one you think has the lowest "1." Just to make things tricky, two of the fractals actually have the same dimension.

⊿ When you are done with your prediction, compute the fractal dimension of each fractal.

⊿ Finally, order these fractals according to their computed dimension. How does your ordering now compare with your intuitive ordering earlier?

a. ____ dim = ____ ____   **b.** ____ dim = ____ ____   **c.** ____ dim = ____ ____

      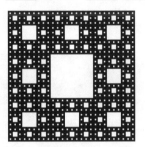

d. ____ dim = ____ ____   **e.** ____ dim = ____ ____   **f.** ____ dim = ____ ____

g. ____ dim = ____ ____   **h.** ____ dim = ____ ____

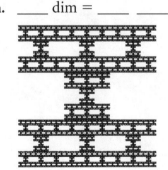

3 ▷ TOPOLOGICAL DIMENSION

Sketch each fractal, then calculate and explain its topological dimension.

a. The Cantor middle-thirds set

_____

_____

_____

_____

_____

b. The Sierpiński tetrahedron

_____

_____

_____

_____

_____

c. The Sierpiński hexagon

_____

_____

_____

_____

_____

4 ▷ THE MENGER SPONGE

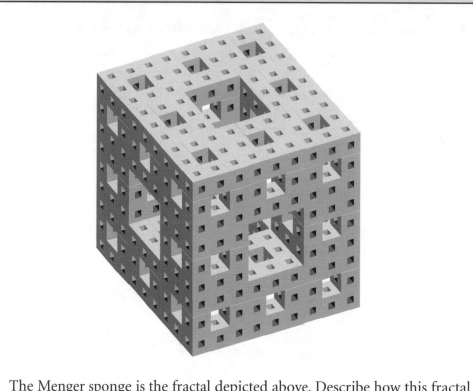

a. The Menger sponge is the fractal depicted above. Describe how this fractal is constructed.

_____

_____

_____

b. Compute its fractal dimension.

_____

_____

_____

c. What is each face of this solid figure called?

_____

_____

_____

5 ▷ THE CANTOR MIDDLE-FIFTHS SET

You construct this set exactly as you did the middle-thirds set except you remove the middle fifth of each interval at each stage of the construction. For example, start with the unit interval $0 \leq x \leq 1$ and remove the middle fifth, leaving behind two intervals: $0 \leq x \leq \frac{2}{5}$ and $\frac{3}{5} \leq x \leq 1$.

a. First sketch and then describe the intervals remaining in this construction at the next stage.

_____

b. Do the same for the following stage.

_____

c. How many pieces does the set contain at stage n of this process?

_____

d. What is the magnification factor of each piece?

_____

e. What is the fractal dimension of the resulting set?

_____

f. Is this dimension larger or smaller than the fractal dimension of the Cantor middle-thirds set? Does this agree with your intuition?

_____

_____

1. Describe a way to construct a set with the fractal dimension of any given number between 0 and 1.

2. Suppose we start with a line segment whose length is 1 and then construct the fractal with the generator shown here.

    Each of the four pieces of the generator has length a, where a is a number between $^1/_4$ and $^1/_2$.

    What is the fractal dimension of this object?

    When $a = ^1/_4$, what is this object? What is its fractal dimension?

    When $a = ^1/_2$, what is this object? What is its fractal dimension?

    If you made a movie and each frame of the film was a picture of this object as a increases, what would you see? Explain in a paragraph or two what the movie would look like.

3. Given any number between 1 and 2, describe a way to construct a fractal whose dimension is exactly that number.

4. What is the dimension of the Sierpiński hexagon? Find two other fractals that have the same dimension but whose appearances are very different.

Natural Fractals

OVERVIEW

This lesson extends the discussion of natural fractals (fractals occurring in nature) versus mathematical fractals. The famous Koch curve fractal is used to help develop concepts related to one of the most obvious natural fractals—coastlines. Students actually compute the fractal dimension of the coastlines of Massachusetts and Maine.

MATHEMATICAL PREREQUISITES

Students need to be familiar with logarithms, graphing, slope, and lines of best fit.

MATHEMATICAL CONNECTIONS

Topics from your mathematics curriculum that have connections to this lesson are concepts of **measurement** and **length**, **lines** and **curves**, and **linearizing data** using **logarithms**. The Lesson Notes below and Answers in the back describe links to more specific concepts and skills.

TECHNOLOGY

Graphing calculators and spreadsheets will be useful for analyzing the data collected as students measure portions of the fractals and coastlines.

SUGGESTED LESSON PLAN

CLASS TIME

One or two 50-minute class periods to explain the graphs and to practice how to actually "measure" the coastline. Students can do additional exercises or projects outside of class.

PREPARATION

Have scissors and paper, card stock, or string ready for students to make rulers for measuring fractals.

LESSON DEVELOPMENT

With these more advanced topics, the lesson development depends greatly on which activities you feel blend best with your curriculum.

LESSON NOTES

After computing the fractal dimensions of the coastlines of Maine and Massachusetts, you might consider having students pick a coastal state, get a map of that state, and compute the fractal dimension of the state's coastline. Rough borders that are not coastlines will work as well.

One of the reasons people have found fractals so interesting is because fractals can be used as mathematical models of many of the complicated shapes that appear in nature. The fractals we have studied so far have some properties which are very similar to those possessed by many natural forms such as coastlines, clouds, trees, and ferns. It is possible to estimate the dimension of fractal-like natural objects as well as fractals. You can do this by estimating the length of the fractal. To see an example, let's examine the Koch curve.

MEASURING THE KOCH CURVE

The Koch curve has several interesting properties. First, it consists of an infinite number of self-similar copies of itself. This includes four copies, each of which is $\frac{1}{3}$ the size of the original. Each of these copies is in turn made up of four copies that are each $\frac{1}{9}$ the size of the original. And each of these copies is made up of four copies $\frac{1}{27}$ the size of the original, and so forth. Look at the image of the Koch curve below to make sure you see this self-similarity.

Second, you may have learned previously that the Koch curve has infinite length. You find this by summing the successively smaller lengths that are added to the shape as you build it. Suppose you were to try to measure this length by hand with a ruler. Since the Koch curve is infinitely squiggly and since rulers come with finite length, you will only be able to approximate the length of the Koch curve. Because of the way you will use your ruler, the approximation you make will depend upon the length of the ruler you choose.

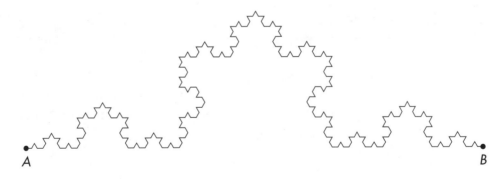

A   B

NAME(S):

Suppose that the Koch curve starts at the point marked *A* and ends at *B* and that the length of segment *AB* is 1 unit. To measure the length of the curve, we would place one end of our ruler at *A* and then swing it around until it intersects the Koch curve again, and then move the ruler to this new starting point and measure again.

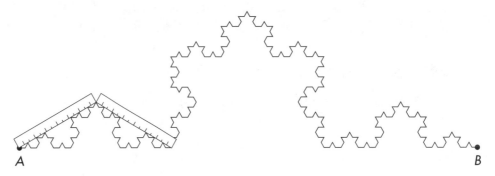

Now if you happened to start with a ruler that was exactly 1 unit long, then the ruler would extend all the way from *A* to *B*, and you might estimate the curve to be 1 unit long.

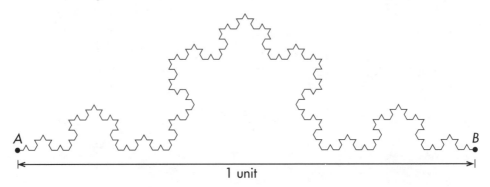

Clearly, we miss a lot of the length of the fractal with this large a ruler, so let's choose a smaller ruler, say $\frac{1}{3}$ unit long. In this case, we find that we need four of these smaller rulers to measure the length of the Koch curve. Note that these four rulers trace out the generator of the Koch curve.

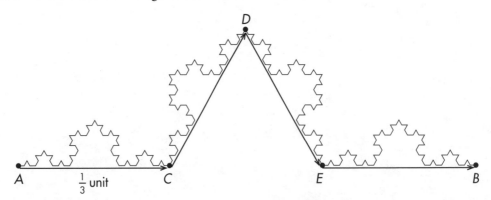

NAME(S):

But again we miss a lot of the nooks and crannies of the Koch curve. If we now choose a smaller ruler, we get a better approximation of the length, but we need to use more rulers. For example, if the ruler length is exactly $\frac{1}{9}$, then we need 16 of these little rulers to measure the Koch curve. These 16 rulers form the second stage in the development of the Koch curve.

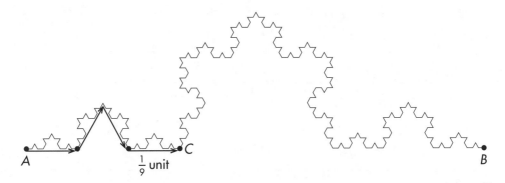

As we see, the smaller the ruler, the more rulers we need to measure the length of the Koch curve.

Ruler length	Number of rulers
1	1
$\frac{1}{3}$	4
$\frac{1}{9} = \left(\frac{1}{3}\right)^2$	$16 = 4^2$
$\frac{1}{27} = \left(\frac{1}{3}\right)^3$	$64 = 4^3$
$\frac{1}{81} = \left(\frac{1}{3}\right)^4$	$256 = 4^4$
$\frac{1}{243} = \left(\frac{1}{3}\right)^5$	$1024 = 4^5$

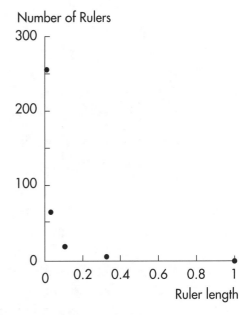

As we see from this table, if we use a ruler whose length is $\frac{1}{3}^n$, then we must use exactly 4^n of these rulers.

In the graph on the right above, we have plotted the number of rulers necessary to measure the Koch curve against the lengths of these rulers. (The numbers from the last row of the table do not appear on the graph.)

NAME(S):

We can see from the previous graph that as the rulers get shorter you need more and more of them. But we already knew that, so this graph doesn't provide much new information. On the other hand, something very interesting happens when you plot the logarithm of the number of rulers against the logarithm of the ruler length.

We first take the logarithm in base 10 of each entry in the table above. (The decimal values in the table are rounded to the nearest hundredth.)

log (Length)	log (Number of rulers)
$\log(1) = 0$	$\log(1) = 0$
$\log\left(\frac{1}{3}\right) = -\log(3) = -0.48$	$\log(4) = 0.60$
$\log\left(\frac{1}{3}\right)^2 = -2\log(3) = -0.95$	$\log\left(4\right)^2 = 2\log(4) = 1.20$
$\log\left(\frac{1}{3}\right)^3 = -3\log(3) = -1.43$	$\log\left(4\right)^3 = 3\log(4) = 1.81$
$-4\log(3) = -1.91$	$4\log(4) = 2.41$
$-5\log(3) = -2.34$	$5\log(4) = 3.01$

The graph of log (Number) vs. log (Length) is linear and its slope is found as follows:

$$\frac{-\log(4)}{\log(3)} \approx -1.26$$

Do you recognize the value of the slope? It is the negative of the fractal dimension of the Koch curve! So this procedure of measuring the length of the curve with smaller and smaller rulers and recording the results is a way to calculate the fractal dimension of a fractal curve.

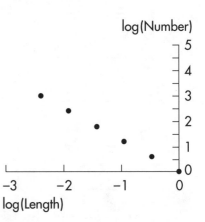

NAME(S):

ANOTHER MATHEMATICAL FRACTAL

Before turning to natural fractals, let's consider a second example of how this works. The first image on the left below shows the generator of another fractal image. It consists of six copies of the (straight-line) generator, each having length $\frac{1}{4}$ the length of the original. So the fractal dimension of the fractal generated by this rule is:

$$\frac{\log(6)}{\log(4)} \approx 1.2924$$

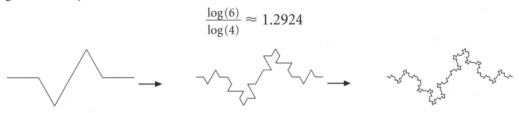

The first few images in the orbit of this geometric iteration are shown above.

Suppose we have only the final image of this fractal (as is the case for natural fractals) and want to know its dimension. We can use our method of measuring with different-sized rulers.

To measure the length of this fractal we start exactly as before, with a ruler of length 1 unit that stretches the length of the generator of this fractal. We need just one of these rulers.

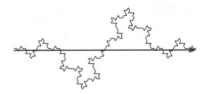

If we choose a ruler of length $\frac{1}{4}$ unit, then we need six rulers to approximate the length.

We can make the following table of ruler lengths and numbers of rulers for this fractal.

Ruler length	Number of rulers
1	1
$\frac{1}{4}$	6
$\frac{1}{4^2}$	6^2
$\frac{1}{4^3}$	6^3

Then we can fill in the corresponding table consisting of the logarithms of the above values.

log (Length)	log (Number of rulers)
$\log(1) = 0$	$\log(1) = 0$
$\log\left(\frac{1}{4}\right) = -\log(4) = -0.6$	$\log(6) = 0.78$
$-2\log(4) = -1.2$	$2\log(6) = 1.56$
$-3\log(4) = -1.8$	$3\log(6) = 2.34$
$-4\log(4) = -2.4$	$4\log(6) = 3.12$

Then finally plot these values on the log-log plot at right.

As before, there is a relationship between the log-log plot and the fractal dimension. The slope of the straight line through these points is exactly $^{-\log 6}/_{\log 4}$, the negative of the fractal dimension.

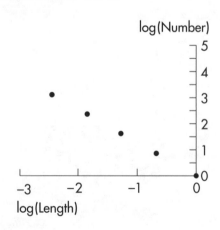

AN EXPERIMENT

Let's now try to approximate the fractal dimension of a fractal using only rulers of differing lengths. Instead of using a fractal whose generator we know, let's look at a more complicated image. Here is a fractal and a ruler of length 1 unit.

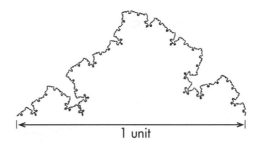

If we measure this fractal using a ruler of length ½ unit, we find that it takes approximately 2.4 rulers to do the job.

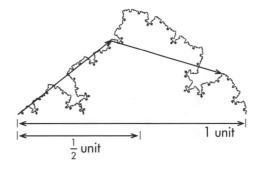

We need approximately 5.9 rulers of size ¼ unit,

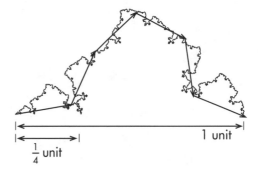

and approximately 15 of length ⅛ unit.

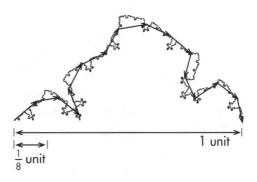

Summarizing this information so far in a table, we find:

Ruler length	Number of rulers
1	1
$\frac{1}{2}$	2.4
$\frac{1}{4}$	5.9
$\frac{1}{8}$	15

or, taking logarithms:

log (Length)	log (Number of rulers)
$\log(1) = 0$	$\log(1) = 0$
$\log\left(\frac{1}{2}\right) = -0.30$	$\log(2.4) = 0.380$
$\log\left(\frac{1}{4}\right) = -0.60$	$\log(5.9) = 0.770$
$\log\left(\frac{1}{8}\right) = -0.90$	$\log(15) = 1.176$

A plot of these four data points is shown at right.

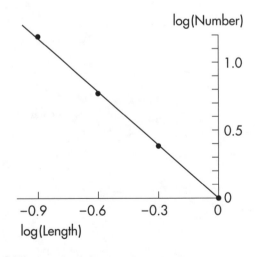

These points do not all lie on a straight line, but they lie fairly close to the line pictured. This line has slope $^{1.15}/_{-0.9} \approx -1.278$. Of course, we could have chosen many other nearby straight lines with different slopes, so we do not get the exact value of the fractal dimension by this method. We only get an approximation, and we conclude that this fractal has dimension approximately 1.278. Notice that this fractal is a little more complex than the Koch curve, so it is not a surprise that its fractal dimension is a little larger.

NAME(S): _____

1 ▷ CUMULUS CLOUD

Graphic designers use fractals like the one below to create images of clouds.

a. Before you make any calculations, estimate the dimension of this cloudlike fractal based on your experience with other fractals. Record your estimate here. _____

Here is a fractal and a segment of length 1 unit. Create your own ruler 1 unit long. Measure the length of this fractal curve using smaller and smaller versions of this ruler, and fill in the following tables. (*Hint:* Make your ruler by cutting a strip of paper 1 unit long. To make a ruler half as long, simply fold your previous ruler in half.) Finally, construct a log-log plot of your data points.

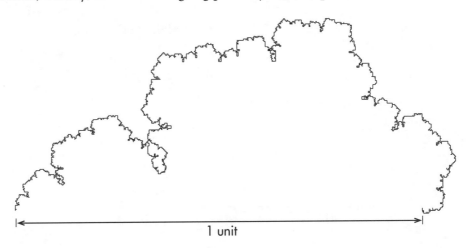

|←————————————— 1 unit —————————————→|

b.

Ruler length	Number of rulers
1	1
$\frac{1}{2}$	
$\frac{1}{4}$	
$\frac{1}{8}$	

c.

log (Length)	log (Number of rulers)
$\log(1) = 0$	$\log(1) = 0$
$\log\left(\frac{1}{2}\right) = -0.30$	
$\log\left(\frac{1}{4}\right) = -0.60$	
$\log\left(\frac{1}{8}\right) = -0.90$	

d.

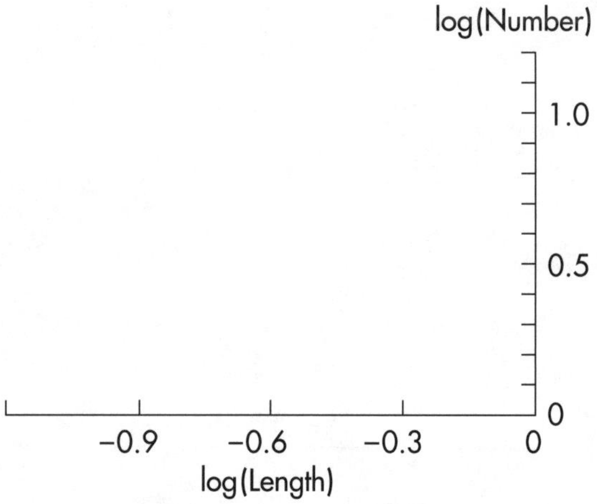

e. Estimate the slope of this straight line to determine an approximation of the dimension.

_____

_____

2 ▷ MORE FRACTALS

Repeat Investigation 1 for each of the following fractals. You might want to estimate the dimensions of all of them first, then divide up the fractals for different people or groups to measure.

TECHNOLOGY TIP

You can collect the information of your ruler lengths and numbers on a graphing calculator or spreadsheet. Then calculate the logarithms of these numbers in separate columns. Finally, graph the data from the columns containing the logarithms. Record or print your data. Adjust the numbers in the original columns to match the next fractal.

Show your work on other sheets of paper.

a. A lightning bolt

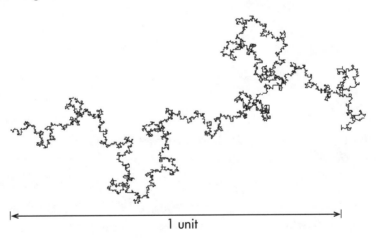

1 unit

b. A Koch-like curve

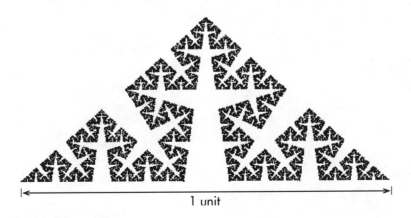

1 unit

c. Another cloud

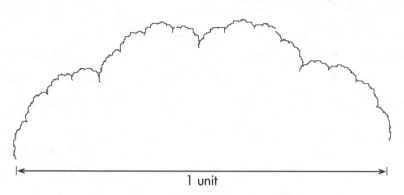

1 unit

3 ▷ A NEW RULER

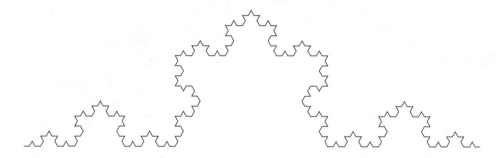

In the Explanation pages we used rulers of length $\frac{1}{3}^n$ above to compute the dimension of the Koch curve because each small piece of the Koch curve was exactly $\frac{1}{3}$ the size of its "parent."

What happens if you instead use rulers of size $\frac{1}{2}^n$ units? That is, repeat the previous investigation on the Koch curve using rulers of this size. Summarize your findings here:

_____

_____

_____

The preceding investigations should convince you of the following: If you measure the length of a fractal curve using a collection of rulers whose lengths get shorter and shorter, and then do a log-log plot of the data (length of ruler versus number of rulers needed), you get a set of points that is almost linear.

If you were to do the same thing with the "fractal-like" object at right, you should get the same result. The figure at right comes from a map of the coast of Maine.

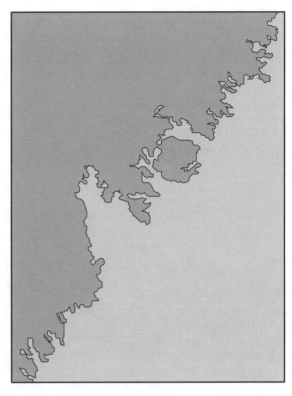

1. Using the method of this section, collect data for the length of the coastline of Maine using rulers of various sizes. Complete tables like those below. Then plot your data from the second table on another sheet of paper. What is the fractal dimension of this coastline?

Ruler length	Number of rulers
1	
$\frac{1}{2}$	
$\frac{1}{4}$	
$\frac{1}{8}$	
$\frac{1}{16}$	

log (Length)	log (Number of rulers)
$\log(1) = 0$	
$\log\left(\frac{1}{2}\right) = -0.30$	
$\log\left(\frac{1}{4}\right) = -0.60$	
$\log\left(\frac{1}{8}\right) = -0.90$	
$\log\left(\frac{1}{16}\right) = -1.2$	

NAME(S): _____

2. Now compute the fractal
   dimension of the coastline
   of Massachusetts. Show and
   explain your work.

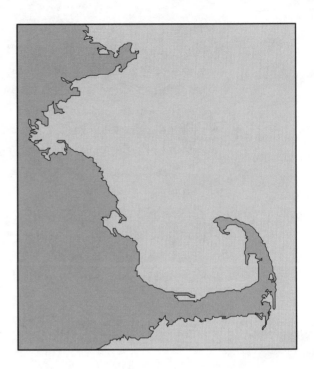

FRACTALS: A TOOL KIT OF DYNAMICS ACTIVITIES
©1999 KEY CURRICULUM PRESS

Areas and Perimeters of Fractals

OVERVIEW

This lesson introduces techniques for computing the perimeter of a fractal and the area bounded by a fractal. The method involves the use of geometric series and leads to some surprising results.

MATHEMATICAL PREREQUISITES

Students need to be able to calculate the perimeter and area of basic geometric figures. Some knowledge of surface area and volume will also be helpful.

MATHEMATICAL CONNECTIONS

Topics from your mathematics curriculum that have connections to this lesson are **exponents** and **geometric series**. Because the lesson actually derives the formula

$$1 + r + r^2 + r^3 + \ldots = \frac{1}{1-r}$$

in the Explanation pages, it might serve as a replacement unit for the equivalent lesson in your regular curriculum. The lesson also works well as an informal introduction to **limits**. The Lesson Notes below and Answers in the back describe links to more specific concepts and skills.

TECHNOLOGY

Students can use graphing calculators to compute perimeter and area for successive iterations, and graph the orbit of these values. You can use a spreadsheet for the same purpose.

SUGGESTED LESSON PLAN

CLASS TIME

You may want to spend one 50-minute class period presenting the explanatory material, then let students spend one to two days working on Investigations and Further Exploration problems. Or, you might choose to have students read the material on their own, then have them work in pairs or groups outside of class on the Investigations.

LESSON NOTES

Make sure students see that a fractal can have infinite perimeter but be the boundary of a region of finite area. This is an essential idea in the lesson.

F ractals are interesting geometric objects in many different ways. In this lesson you will see that fractals often have geometric properties that are very different from the corresponding properties in Euclidean geometry. In particular, the perimeters and areas of fractal objects may surprise you.

LENGTH OF THE KOCH CURVE

Let's begin by computing the length of the Koch curve. This is a fairly complicated curve, but we can still compute its length. We do this one stage at a time, because each stage of the construction consists of a collection of straight line segments whose lengths we know. If we start with a generator of 1 unit length, then there are 4 segments of length $\frac{1}{3}$ in the figure at stage 1, 16 segments of length $\frac{1}{9}$ at stage 2, and so forth. Let's make a table of the number of segments and the lengths at various stages.

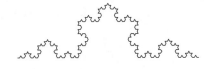

Stage	Number of segments	Image	Length of each segment	Total length (in linear units)
0	1		1	1
1	4		$\frac{1}{3}$	$4 \cdot \frac{1}{3} = \frac{4}{3} = 1.333\ldots$
2	$16 = 4^2$		$\frac{1}{9} = \left(\frac{1}{3}\right)^2$	$16 \cdot \frac{1}{9} = \frac{16}{9} = 1.777\ldots$
3	$64 = 4^3$		$\frac{1}{27} = \left(\frac{1}{3}\right)^3$	$4^3 \cdot \frac{1}{3^3} = \left(\frac{4}{3}\right)^3 = 2.370\ldots$
4	$256 = 4^4$		$\frac{1}{81} = \left(\frac{1}{3}\right)^4$	$\left(\frac{4}{3}\right)^4 = 3.160\ldots$

After iterating this rule infinitely many times, we obtain the Koch curve.

Notice what is happening in the last column. The linear measure of the curve is getting larger at each stage. If we continue to add entries to that column we get:

Length at stage 5: $\left(\frac{4}{3}\right)^5 = 4.214\ldots$

Length at stage 6: $\left(\frac{4}{3}\right)^6 = 5.619\ldots$

Length at stage 7: $\left(\frac{4}{3}\right)^7 = 7.492\ldots$

Length at stage 8: $\left(\frac{4}{3}\right)^8 = 9.989\ldots$

Length at stage 9: $\left(\frac{4}{3}\right)^9 = 13.318\ldots$

Length at stage 10: $\left(\frac{4}{3}\right)^{10} = 17.757\ldots$

The length of this curve at the nth stage is given by the formula:

$$\text{Length at stage } n = \left(\frac{4}{3}\right)^n$$

Each time we pass to a new stage in the construction of the Koch curve, the length increases by a factor of $\frac{4}{3}$. So the length just keeps increasing without bound. The Koch curve is infinitely long!

AREA UNDER THE KOCH CURVE

But now consider the area underneath the Koch curve. By area "underneath" we really mean the area between the Koch curve at stage infinity and the Koch curve at stage 0. This area must be finite, because the area must be smaller than the area of this page. So if we look at the Koch snowflake, we have found a figure whose perimeter is infinite but whose area is finite. Fractals can have some very strange properties!

Not only is the area under the Koch curve finite, but we can compute it exactly. The area is the sum of the areas of the small triangles that we add at each stage of the construction. At the initial stage we have just a straight line, so there is no area. But at stage 1, we have a single equilateral triangle.

We could compute this area exactly, since we know the dimensions of the equilateral triangle. But let's not bother at this point. Rather, let's just call the area of this triangle A and work with that variable quantity instead.

At stage 2, we have four additional triangles.

Each of these new triangles has base and height that are $\frac{1}{3}$ the size of the original triangle. Therefore, each of these triangles has area that is $\frac{1}{9}$ the area of the first triangle, or $\left(\frac{1}{9}\right)A$. (Since there are four of them, we find that the area at the second stage is given by:

$$A + \frac{4}{9}A$$

At the next stage we add 16 smaller triangles whose dimensions are now $\frac{1}{81}$ the size of the original triangle. Therefore the area of each of these triangles is $\left(\frac{1}{81}\right)A$ and the area at this stage is:

$$A + \frac{4}{9}A + \frac{16}{81}A$$

With an eye toward what comes later, we can rewrite this sum as:

$$A + \frac{4}{9}A + \left(\frac{4}{9}\right)^2 A$$

At stage 3, we add 4^3 triangles, each with area $\left(\frac{1}{9}\right)^3 A$, so our area becomes:

$$A + \frac{4}{9}A + \left(\frac{4}{9}\right)^2 A + \left(\frac{4}{9}\right)^3 A$$

The pattern is now clear. At the nth stage we must compute:

$$A + \frac{4}{9}A + \left(\frac{4}{9}\right)^2 A + \left(\frac{4}{9}\right)^3 A + \cdots + \left(\frac{4}{9}\right)^n A$$

Factoring out the A, we have:

$$A\left[1 + \frac{4}{9} + \left(\frac{4}{9}\right)^2 + \left(\frac{4}{9}\right)^3 + \cdots + \left(\frac{4}{9}\right)^n\right]$$

This partial sum seems unwieldy enough. However, we want to compute the **infinite** sum:

$$A\left[1 + \frac{4}{9} + \left(\frac{4}{9}\right)^2 + \left(\frac{4}{9}\right)^3 + \cdots + \left(\frac{4}{9}\right)^n + \cdots\right]$$

It seems that adding up infinitely many terms would take us infinitely long. Luckily, a tried and true process of mathematics comes to the rescue. There is a neat way to add up an infinite sum of the form

$$1 + r + r^2 + r^3 + \cdots$$

where r is a positive number less than 1. So let's take a detour and figure this out and then return to the area problem.

THE GEOMETRIC SERIES

An infinite sum of the form

$$1 + r + r^2 + r^3 + \cdots$$

is called a **geometric series**. It turns out that this type of sum arises in many different areas of mathematics, particularly in applications that require the use of calculus. We do not need calculus to compute this sum, however. For example, consider the following scenario.

You are standing on the real number line at the number 0, minding your own business, when we tell you to go half the distance to the number 2. You obligingly move 1 unit toward 2. So you have exactly 1 unit left to travel if you want to go all the way to 2. Now we again tell you to move half the distance to 2. You hit the road again and move $\frac{1}{2}$ unit more, ending up at $\frac{3}{2}$. You now have $\frac{1}{2}$ unit left to travel. When we say it again, you move $\frac{1}{4}$ unit toward 2—ending up at $\frac{7}{4}$, and leaving you with $\frac{1}{4}$ unit to travel. And so forth. Here is the picture of your travels:

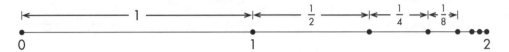

The distance you travel is just the geometric series with $r = \frac{1}{2}$ and the first term of 1:

$$1 + \frac{1}{2} + \left(\frac{1}{2}\right)^2 + \left(\frac{1}{2}\right)^3 + \left(\frac{1}{2}\right)^4 + \cdots$$

From the picture above, we see that as we add more and more terms to this sum, we come closer and closer to 2. Now we never get larger than 2, so it makes sense to say that the infinite sum actually is 2. That is, for this geometric series with $r = \frac{1}{2}$:

$$1 + \frac{1}{2} + \left(\frac{1}{2}\right)^2 + \left(\frac{1}{2}\right)^3 + \left(\frac{1}{2}\right)^4 + \cdots = 2$$

Well, that takes care of the case of $r = \frac{1}{2}$, but what about the general case? First of all, let's notice that if $r = 1$, the sum of the first n 1's is simply n, since $1 + 1 + 1 + \cdots + 1 = n$. Because we can make this sum as large as we want by simply adding up enough 1's, the sum is infinity. The same is true if r is larger than 1, so we see that the geometric series adds up to infinity if r is 1 or larger.

$$\text{when } r = 1, \quad 1 + 1 + 1 + 1 + 1 + \cdots = \infty$$

$$\text{when } r > 1, \quad 1 + r + r^2 + r^3 + r^4 + \cdots = \infty$$

To handle other cases—that is, when $r < 1$ $\left(\text{besides } r = \frac{1}{2}\right)$ we use a little trick. Let's multiply the sum $1 + r + r^2 + r^3 + \cdots + r^n$ by $1 - r$. We compute:

$$\left(1 + r + r^2 + r^3 + \cdots + r^n\right)(1 - r)$$

$$= 1(1 - r) + r(1 - r) + r^2(1 - r) + r^3(1 - r) + \cdots + r^n(1 - r)$$

$$= 1 - r \quad + r - r^2 \quad + r^2 - r^3 \quad + r^3 - \cdots - r^n + \quad r^n - r^{n+1}$$

Almost all the terms drop out, giving us

$$= 1 - r^{n+1}$$

Dividing by $(1 - r)$, we then find:

$$1 + r + r^2 + r^3 + \cdots + r^n = \frac{1 - r^{n+1}}{1 - r}$$

So this gives us a neat little formula for adding up the first n powers of r. How does this help? Well, remember that r is between 0 and 1. So the number r^{n+1} gets smaller and smaller as n gets larger. For example, if $r = 0.1$, then $r^9 = 0.000000001$, which is pretty small; and r^{100} features 99 zeros after the decimal point, which is tinier still. So we see that the number r^{n+1} tends to 0 as n gets larger and larger. As we continue to add more and more terms to the sum, this term tends to "disappear" and we are left with just $\frac{1}{(1 - r)}$. That is, we can say:

$$1 + r + r^2 + r^3 + \cdots = \frac{1}{1 - r}$$

So it is easy to add up the infinitely many terms in the geometric series. The total is just $\frac{1}{(1 - r)}$. Neat, huh?

Of course, you are probably saying, "How did anyone ever come up with that little trick? I never could have." Well, don't be so sure. Mathematicians have been working on problems like this for over 2,000 years. If you had 2,000 years to come up with this sum, you probably could have done it too!

Let's check this formula with the known case when $r = \frac{1}{2}$. We find:

$$1 + \frac{1}{2} + \left(\frac{1}{2}\right)^2 + \left(\frac{1}{2}\right)^3 + \left(\frac{1}{2}\right)^4 + \cdots = \frac{1}{1 - \frac{1}{2}} = \frac{1}{\frac{1}{2}} = 2$$

Yes, it works! That's just what we found before.

You will use this formula to finish finding the area under the Koch curve in Investigation 2.

1 ▹ SUM SOME SERIES

Add up each of the following expressions:

a. $1 + \frac{1}{3} + \left(\frac{1}{3}\right)^2 + \left(\frac{1}{3}\right)^3 + \left(\frac{1}{3}\right)^4 + \cdots = $ _____

b. $1 + \frac{2}{5} + \left(\frac{2}{5}\right)^2 + \left(\frac{2}{5}\right)^3 + \left(\frac{2}{5}\right)^4 + \cdots = $ _____

c. $1 + \frac{3}{2} + \left(\frac{3}{2}\right)^2 + \left(\frac{3}{2}\right)^3 + \left(\frac{3}{2}\right)^4 + \cdots = $ _____

d. $\frac{3}{4} + \left(\frac{3}{4}\right)^2 + \left(\frac{3}{4}\right)^3 + \left(\frac{3}{4}\right)^4 + \cdots = $ _____

e. $1 + \left(\frac{1}{3}\right)^2 + \left(\frac{1}{3}\right)^4 + \left(\frac{1}{3}\right)^6 + \cdots = $ _____

f. $1 + \frac{2}{3} + \frac{2}{9} + \frac{2}{27} + \frac{2}{81} + \cdots = $ _____

2 ▹ THE AREA UNDER THE KOCH CURVE

Compute the area under the Koch curve. You may assume that the equilateral triangle at stage 1 has area A.

$$A\left[1 + \frac{4}{9} + \left(\frac{4}{9}\right)^2 + \left(\frac{4}{9}\right)^3 + \left(\frac{4}{9}\right)^4 + \cdots\right] = \underline{\hspace{4cm}}$$

3 ▹ THE LENGTH OF THE KOCH CURVE

a. How many stages of the construction of the Koch curve would you have to perform to guarantee that the length at this stage is larger than 100 units? Explain your answer.

_____

b. Larger than 200 units? _____

TECHNOLOGY TIP

Many calculators allow you to iterate on the result of a previous calculation by repeatedly pressing the "enter" or "=" key. This feature may help you with some of your work in this lesson.

FRACTALS: A TOOL KIT OF DYNAMICS ACTIVITIES
©1999 KEY CURRICULUM PRESS

4 ▷ AREA OF THE SIERPIŃSKI TRIANGLE

Let's try to figure out the area of the Sierpiński triangle. Before we begin, let's think a bit. In the construction of this fractal by removals, we successively remove "middle triangles" at each stage of the construction. By the time we iterate this procedure infinitely often, we remove virtually everything from the original triangle, so it looks like the area of the triangle should be 0. That is by no means a proof of this fact. It's only our intuition. So let's see if we are correct.

To compute the area of the Sierpiński triangle, let's suppose that the area of our original triangle is 1 and we proceed just as we did above with the Koch curve. At the initial stage our area is 1. But then we remove a single triangle whose area is $\frac{1}{4}$ of the entire area, so we remove area $\frac{1}{4}$ at the first stage. The chart below contains this information.

a. Complete the chart. (You do not need to create the missing images.)

Stage	Number of triangles removed	Image	Area of each triangle removed	Total area removed at this stage	Total area removed so far
0	0	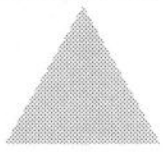	none	none	none
1	1		$\frac{1}{4}$	$\frac{1}{4}$	$\frac{1}{4}$
2	3	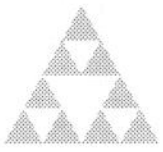	$\frac{1}{16} = \left(\frac{1}{4}\right)^2$	$3\left(\frac{1}{4}\right)^2$	$\frac{1}{4} + 3\left(\frac{1}{4}\right)^2$
3					
4					
n					

b. The area of the Sierpiński triangle is _____ because:

_____

_____

5 ▷ PERIMETER OF THE SIERPIŃSKI TRIANGLE

Now let's calculate the perimeter of the Sierpiński triangle. The first question is: What exactly do we mean by the perimeter of this object? Recall that the boundary of each removed triangle in the construction remains and so forms a part of the final triangle. These lines form the interior boundary of the Sierpiński triangle and so make up part of the perimeter. Therefore we can calculate the perimeter at each stage and then see what happens as the stage number increases. At the first stage we have simply an equilateral triangle whose side is, say, S. (We use it so we don't get involved with any nasty numbers.) At the second stage, more of the perimeter appears. We add three new line segments to the perimeter, and each has length $S/2$.

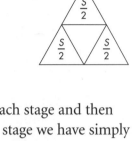

a. First fill in the following table:

Stage	Number of sides added	Image	Length of each added side	Total length added at this stage	Total length added so far
0	none		none	none	$3S$
1	3		$\dfrac{S}{2}$	$\dfrac{3S}{2}$	$3S + \dfrac{3S}{2}$
2					
3					
4					
n					

b. Conclusion: Do you see the pattern? What is happening to the perimeter of the Sierpiński triangle?

_____

_____

_____

Fractals sure are strange objects!

NAME(S):

1. Calculate the length of the Cantor middle-thirds set. Do this by subtracting the total length of the segments that are removed at each iteration.

Cantor middle-thirds set

2. Calculate the area of the Sierpiński carpet. Compare this area to that of the Sierpiński triangle.

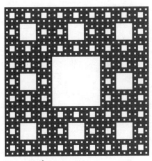

Sierpiński carpet

3. Consider the fractal whose generator is

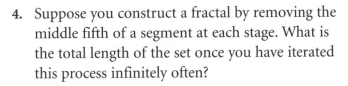

where the original length is 1 and each of the segments in the generator has length ²⁄₅. What is the area under the resulting fractal? Why?

4. Suppose you construct a fractal by removing the middle fifth of a segment at each stage. What is the total length of the set once you have iterated this process infinitely often?

5. Show that the Sierpiński tetrahedron has volume equal to 0 and finite surface area. Also find its surface area if the original tetrahedron has surface area S.

Sierpiński tetrahedron

6. Show that the Menger sponge has volume equal to 0 but infinite surface area.

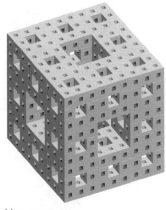

Menger sponge

Decoding the Cantor Set

OVERVIEW

This lesson contains a fascinating study of the Cantor set. Students learn an algorithm that identifies whether points within the Cantor set are endpoints of segments. Contrary to first notions, the Cantor set is not made up simply of a bunch of endpoints of the "remaining" segments. Using similar reasoning, the lesson explores which points lie on the vertices of the removed triangles in the Sierpiński triangle. In the last Further Exploration problem, students discover the winning strategy for the "target practice" chaos game first introduced in Lesson 5, Random Iteration: The Chaos Game.

MATHEMATICAL PREREQUISITES

Students need to be familiar with geometric series.

MATHEMATICAL CONNECTIONS

This lesson connects with the topics of **binary arithmetic** and **infinite series** and **sequences** and is a nice introduction to **limits** and some basic ideas of **number theory**.

LESSON NOTES

Further Exploration problem 3 revisits the "target practice" problem from the chaos game and gives a hint toward relating your strategy for the game to the coding developed in this lesson.

This lesson might be used as an extended project or independent study project where a student could learn the material on his or her own, then teach it to the class.

Another way to use this lesson is to present the basic concepts to the class, then have students select an Investigation or Further Exploration problem to prepare as a project for a final presentation.

When you first see the Cantor middle-thirds set, it does not appear to be the most engaging of fractals. In fact, it looks more or less like a scatter of dust on the real number line. But when you look more closely at the Cantor set, you see that there is much more than meets the eye.

Recall how the Cantor set is constructed. We start with the interval $0 \leq x \leq 1$ and then remove every middle-third interval that we encounter. Here is the picture:

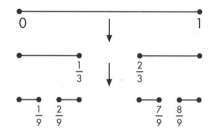

Remember that we leave behind the endpoints of each interval that is removed, so numbers like 0, 1, $\frac{1}{3}$, $\frac{2}{3}$, $\frac{1}{9}$, and so forth remain behind and are therefore part of the Cantor set. This happens because, as we successively remove intervals further along in this process, these removed intervals never include the prior endpoints.

So, at first glance, it would seem that the Cantor set is just a collection of endpoints. But it turns out that this hunch is completely wrong. In fact, the endpoints comprise just a tiny portion of the points that actually reside in the Cantor set.

To understand this, let's identify points in the Cantor set in a completely different way. We'll give a code name to each point and then use this code to identify exactly which point we are talking about. This is like real life. We authors call ourselves Alice, Bob, and Jon. But the U.S. government knows us by our Social Security numbers. These are our "code names" as far as the government is concerned, and the government has a way of going from our Social Security numbers to our real names. We'll apply a similar procedure here.

CODING THE CANTOR SET

To attach a code name to any point in the Cantor set, note that we can identify each point by telling in which of two intervals the point lies at each stage of the construction—the left interval or the right interval. So our code names will consist of a string of L's and R's, indicating the left or right interval in which the given member of the Cantor set resides at each stage of the construction. In a sense, the code name describes the address of each resident of the Cantor set.

For example, the code name attached to 0 is LLLLLL . . . , an infinite string of all L's. This is because 0 lies in the left-hand interval at each stage of the construction:

In a similar fashion, the address of 1 is RRRR . . . , all right-hand intervals. How about ⅓?

Well, ⅓ lies in the initial left interval, but thereafter lies in all rights, so the code for ⅓ is LRRRR . . . .

Similarly, the code for ⅔ is RLLLLL . . . .

Do you notice something? Each of these codes ends in an infinite string of either all L's or all R's. In fact, that's always true. An endpoint in the Cantor set has a code name that begins with some finite string of L's and R's, but then ends in an infinite string of either all L's or all R's (see Investigation 1). That's the key to understanding why there are so many non-endpoints in the Cantor set. Any infinite string of L's and R's specifies a perfectly good point in the Cantor set, but as long as its "tail" is not all L's or all R's, it cannot be an endpoint.

For example, think about the repeating sequence LRLRLR . . . . That specifies a point in the Cantor set as shown in the figure on the right.

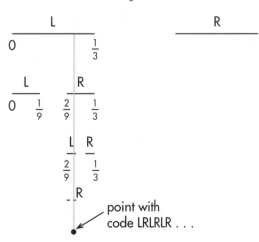

point with code LRLRLR . . .

NAME(S):

So there are lots of non-endpoints in the Cantor set. For example, the point with code RLRLRL . . . must also be there. So too must

$$\text{LLRLLRLLR} \ldots$$

$$\text{RLR RLR RLR} \ldots$$

$$\text{RRRL RRRL RRRL} \ldots$$

and on and on. All of these sequences have repeating code names, but a code name need not repeat. For example, the code name

$$\text{RL RRL RRRL RRRRL RRRRRL} \ldots$$

never repeats. But it also does not end in an infinite string of L's or R's. So it corresponds to some point in the Cantor set that is not an endpoint.

UNTANGLING THE CODE

Given any point in the Cantor set, we have attached an infinite set of L's and R's to identify this point. That is all well and good, but how do we use our knowledge of the code to describe these points as numbers along the number line in the ordinary way? There is a neat way of doing this that involves the geometric series that we discussed before. Given a particular code involving L's and R's, we first write down a geometric series whose numerators are the L's and R's that comprise the code in exact order and whose denominators are powers of 3. For example, if our code is LRLRLR . . . , we first write

$$\frac{L}{3} + \frac{R}{3^2} + \frac{L}{3^3} + \frac{R}{3^4} + \frac{L}{3^5} + \frac{R}{3^6} + \cdots$$

Note that we do not include the constant term 1. Now we change every L to a 0 and every R to a 2, and we have a geometric series that we can sum. The result of this addition is precisely the number whose code we started with!

Let's check this with a few examples. Suppose our code is LLLL . . . . Well, of course we know that this code corresponds to 0, but let's see what the geometric series gives. We first write

$$\frac{L}{3} + \frac{L}{3^2} + \frac{L}{3^3} + \frac{L}{3^4} + \frac{L}{3^5} + \frac{L}{3^6} + \cdots$$

and then change each L to 0. Then each term in the sum is 0, so the entire sum is 0, just as we would expect.

If our sequence is RRR . . . , its geometric series should correspond to 1. In our infinite sum, each numerator R becomes 2, so we must add up:

$$\frac{2}{3} + \frac{2}{3^2} + \frac{2}{3^3} + \frac{2}{3^4} + \frac{2}{3^5} + \frac{2}{3^6} + \cdots$$

Factoring out $\frac{2}{3}$ from each term, we are left with:

$$\frac{2}{3}\left(1 + \frac{1}{3} + \frac{1}{3^2} + \frac{1}{3^3} + \frac{1}{3^4} + \frac{1}{3^5} + \frac{1}{3^6} + \cdots\right)$$

Within the parentheses is the basic geometric series with a common ratio of $\frac{1}{3}$. This sums to:

$$\frac{1}{1 - \frac{1}{3}} = \frac{1}{\frac{2}{3}} = \frac{3}{2}$$

Multiplying by $\frac{2}{3}$ then gives the expected result, namely 1.

If we begin with the sequence RLLLL . . . that corresponds to $\frac{2}{3}$, we write

$$\frac{R}{3} + \frac{L}{3^2} + \frac{L}{3^3} + \frac{L}{3^4} + \frac{L}{3^5} + \frac{L}{3^6} + \cdots$$

Changing each L to 0 and each R to 2 gives the result $\frac{2}{3}$ right away. The sequence for $\frac{1}{3}$, LRRRR . . . , needs more work to verify. We have

$$\frac{L}{3} + \frac{R}{3^2} + \frac{R}{3^3} + \frac{R}{3^4} + \frac{R}{3^5} + \frac{R}{3^6} + \cdots$$

which becomes

$$\frac{0}{3} + \frac{2}{3^2} + \frac{2}{3^3} + \frac{2}{3^4} + \frac{2}{3^5} + \frac{2}{3^6} + \cdots$$

$$= \frac{2}{9}\left(1 + \frac{1}{3} + \frac{1}{3^2} + \frac{1}{3^3} + \frac{1}{3^4} + \frac{1}{3^5} + \frac{1}{3^6} + \cdots\right)$$

$$= \frac{2}{9}\left(\frac{1}{1 - \frac{1}{3}}\right) = \frac{2}{9} \cdot \frac{3}{2} = \frac{1}{3}$$

Now let's try a non-endpoint such as LRLRLR . . . . We first write

$$\frac{L}{3} + \frac{R}{3^2} + \frac{L}{3^3} + \frac{R}{3^4} + \frac{L}{3^5} + \frac{R}{3^6} + \cdots$$

which becomes:

$$\frac{0}{3} + \frac{2}{3^2} + \frac{0}{3^3} + \frac{2}{3^4} + \frac{0}{3^5} + \frac{2}{3^6} + \cdots$$

$$= \frac{2}{3^2} + \frac{2}{3^4} + \frac{2}{3^6} + \frac{2}{3^8} + \cdots$$

$$= \frac{2}{9}\left(1 + \frac{1}{9} + \frac{1}{9^2} + \frac{1}{9^3} + \frac{1}{9^4} + \cdots\right)$$

$$= \frac{2}{9}\left(\frac{1}{1 - \frac{1}{9}}\right) = \frac{2}{9} \cdot \frac{9}{8} = \frac{1}{4}$$

So $\frac{1}{4}$ is a member of the Cantor set, but $\frac{1}{4}$ is not an endpoint.

1 ▷ DECODING THE ENDPOINTS

_____   _____   _____   _____
0   1

At the second stage of the construction of the Cantor set, the new endpoints are $\frac{1}{9}$, $\frac{2}{9}$, $\frac{7}{9}$, and $\frac{8}{9}$. List the codes attached to these endpoints:

a. $\frac{1}{9}$: _____

b. $\frac{2}{9}$: _____

c. $\frac{7}{9}$: _____

d. $\frac{8}{9}$: _____

___ ___   ___ ___   ___ ___   ___ ___
0   1

At the next stage of the construction, there are eight new endpoints. List each one together with its code name:

e. ____ Code: _____   ____ Code: _____

____ Code: _____   ____ Code: _____

____ Code: _____   ____ Code: _____

____ Code: _____   ____ Code: _____

-- --   -- --   -- --   -- --
0   1

Here are two endpoints from the next stage. Find their code names.

f. 20/81: Code: _____

g. 26/81: Code: _____

2 ▷ POINTS THAT ARE NOT ENDPOINTS

Write down three different code names that never repeat and so do not correspond to *endpoints* of the Cantor set.

_____

_____

_____

3 ▷ SELF-SIMILARITY

Using the code names, we can see in a very different way the self-similarity of the Cantor set. Consider the two endpoints of an interval that remains behind at the nth stage of the construction. The codes for these two endpoints begin with an identical sequence of L's and R's, but then one of them ends with a tail of all L's and the other ends with a tail of all R's. For example, at the first stage, one of the intervals has endpoints ⅔ and 1. The respective codes are RLLLLL . . . and RRRRRR . . . . Both of these codes begin with an R, but then have opposite tails. At the next stage, one of the intervals has endpoints ⅔ and ⁷⁄₉. These codes are RLLLLL . . . and RLRRRR . . . . Here, both codes begin with an RL but end with opposite tails.

— —   — —   — —   — —
0   1

a. There are eight intervals that remain behind at the third stage of the construction of the Cantor set. List the endpoints and their respective codes for each of these intervals.

1. _____

2. _____

3. _____

4. _____

5. _____

6. _____

7. _____

8. _____

The important consequence of this observation is that any sequence that begins with the same initial L's and R's as the endpoints of one of these intervals must lie in that interval. For example, you saw above that LRLLLLL . . . and LRLRRRR . . . are codes for the endpoints of one of the intervals left after stage 3. Every point in the Cantor set that lies in this interval must begin with LRL. But now we can add *any* sequence of L's and R's whatsoever after the initial LRL. This means that the piece of the Cantor set in this small interval has exactly the same number of points as the entire Cantor set, and moreover, the L and R structure of both the tiny piece and the whole Cantor set is exactly the same.

b. Explain how this is another way of viewing the self-similarity of the Cantor set.

_____

4 ▷ DECODE THE CODE

Write down the number in the Cantor set that corresponds to each of the following code names:

a. RR LLLL . . . _____

b. LL RRRR . . . _____

c. RLR LLLL . . . _____

d. RL RL RL . . . _____

e. RLL RLL RLL . . . _____

f. RR LR LR LR . . . _____

5 ▷ DECODING THE SIERPIŃSKI TRIANGLE

We can assign similar codes to many fractals. For example, we can assign a code involving the three letters U (upper), L (left), and R (right) to any point in the Sierpiński triangle. At the first stage, we assign the U, L, or R depending upon which initial triangle our point lives in. We do not assign any code to the vacant central triangle, since there are no points of the Sierpiński triangle in this region.

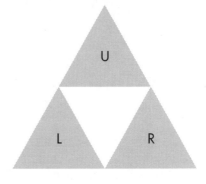

At the second stage, we continue just as in the Cantor set. All points in the upper triangle have first letter U, since they live in the upper triangle. But then their second letter depends upon which smaller triangle they live in.

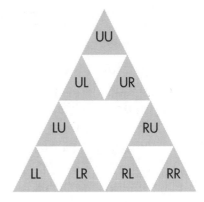

Here is a picture of the next stage in the construction of the Sierpiński triangle. Indicate on this picture the first three letters in the address of each small triangle.

---

6 ▷ DECODING THE VERTICES

a. What is the (infinitely long) code name associated with each of the following points in the Sierpiński triangle?

$A =$ _____

$B =$ _____

$C =$ _____

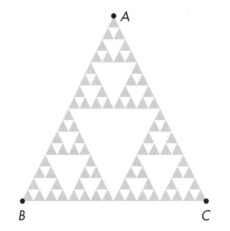

b. Unlike the Cantor set, some points in the Sierpiński triangle have two codes associated with them. For example, each of the following points has two code names. List them.

$A = $ _____

$B = $ _____

$C = $ _____

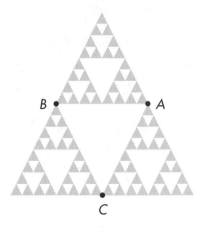

c. Same question here: List the code names for each indicated point.

$A = $ _____

$B = $ _____

$C = $ _____

$D = $ _____

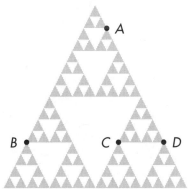

d. Based on the information from the beginning of this Investigation, describe the code names for any point that lies at a vertex of a small vacant triangle in the Sierpiński triangle.

_____

_____

_____

_____

FRACTALS: A TOOL KIT OF DYNAMICS ACTIVITIES
©1999 KEY CURRICULUM PRESS

1. Discuss this statement: Most of the points in the Sierpiński triangle do not lie on a vertex of a small, removed triangle.

2. Describe the code names of the points that lie on the base of the Sierpiński triangle. If you change L's to 0's and R's to 1's, do you see any relationship between this code and binary numbers (assuming the base is the interval $0 \leq x \leq 1$)?

3. Find the relationship between the code names you assign to regions of the Sierpiński triangle and the "target practice" game we played in Lesson 5, Random Iteration: The Chaos Game.

TECHNOLOGY TIP

To play the chaos game on the Web, visit the following Web site:

http://math.bu.edu//DYSYS/applets.

Answers

LESSON 1 ▷ GEOMETRIC ITERATION

INVESTIGATION 1: A SHRINKING ITERATION RULE

a.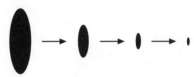

b. Possible answer:

c. The orbit tends to a single point.

d. The orbit tends to just one point even though there are two lines. The picture is squeezed in both the horizontal direction and the vertical direction, making the two lines come closer and closer as they grow smaller and smaller.

INVESTIGATION 2: A ROTATING ITERATION RULE

a.

The square is fixed for this orbit; the picture never changes.

b.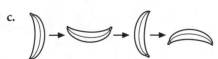

The orbit is a cycle of period 2.

c.

The orbit is a cycle of period 4.

INVESTIGATION 3: A MIDPOINT ITERATION RULE

a.

The orbit is approaching a single point.

b.

	Original square (the seed)	First iteration	Second iteration	Third iteration	nth iteration in the orbit
Side length (in units)	1	$\frac{1}{\sqrt{2}}$	$\frac{1}{2}$ or $\left(\frac{1}{\sqrt{2}}\right)^2$	$\frac{1}{2\sqrt{2}}$ or $\left(\frac{1}{\sqrt{2}}\right)^3$	$\left(\frac{1}{\sqrt{2}}\right)^n$
Area (in square units)	1	$\frac{1}{2}$	$\frac{1}{4}$	$\frac{1}{8}$	$\left(\frac{1}{2}\right)^n$

INVESTIGATION 4: A REPLACEMENT ITERATION RULE

a.  This orbit is tending to a straight line segment whose length is the diameter of the original circle.

b. If the seed is a square or a rectangle, the fate is the same as in (a): a straight line segment, for which the length is the base of the square or rectangle, respectively. In the case of a stick figure, the orbit tends again to a straight line segment whose length is the greatest width across the original stick figure (e.g., the width between the feet).

INVESTIGATION 5: FAMOUS FRACTAL 1

a. and **b.**

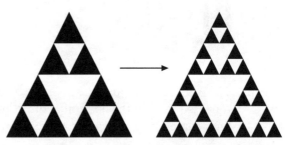

c. The resulting figure contains all of the points on the perimeter of the original triangle as well as each point on the perimeter of any removed triangle. It is essential that students understand this construction. In particular, they need to be able to visualize the next figure in the orbit.

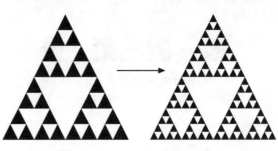

After infinitely many steps, we have removed the middles of all triangles. What remains is a very complicated figure known as a Sierpiński triangle. Here is a picture of the limiting shape:

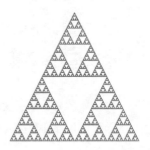

This figure is named for the Polish mathematician Waclaw Sierpiński, who discovered it in the early 1900s. The Sierpiński triangle is one of the most important fractals, one to which we will often return. You will learn more about fractals in later sections.

Incidentally, there are points that remain after we have iterated this process infinitely often. For example, all of the points on the boundary of the original triangle are untouched by this process, and so they are part of the Sierpiński triangle. Similarly, the boundary of any black triangle at an intermediate stage of the construction also remains behind and forms a piece of the Sierpiński triangle.

d.

	Original triangle (the seed)	First iteration	Second iteration	Third iteration	nth iteration
Total number of triangles remaining	1	3	9	27	3^n
Side length of each triangle	1	$\frac{1}{2}$	$\frac{1}{4}$	$\frac{1}{8}$	$\left(\frac{1}{2}\right)^n$

INVESTIGATION 6: FAMOUS FRACTAL 2

a.

b. The Cantor middle-thirds set is named after the German mathematician Georg Cantor who first studied this and similar objects around 1870. It consists of a "dust" of points which contains all of the endpoints of the removed intervals.

c.

	Original segment (the seed)	First iteration	Second iteration	Third iteration	Any iteration in the orbit
Total number of segments	1	2	4	8	2^n
Length of each segment	1	$\frac{1}{3}$	$\frac{1}{9}$	$\frac{1}{27}$	$\left(\frac{1}{3}\right)^n$

d. Infinitely many points remain in the orbit for all iterations, and they are not all endpoints of removed intervals. The Cantor set actually contains *many* more points than the endpoints, but that is by no means clear. In fact, it is just this fact that drove Cantor crazy in the nineteenth century! This is studied further in Lesson 12: Decoding the Cantor Set.

FURTHER EXPLORATION

1. The orbit is:

Only the solid black triangles represent figures in the orbit. We have retained the prior piece of the orbit only to indicate how the next triangle is constructed from the previous one.

Technology Tip: This can be shown with a Geometer's Sketchpad script.

The fate of this orbit is: it tends to a single point. An interesting connection for geometry students to see is that this point is actually the centroid of the original triangle. To see this, simply draw the medians of the original triangle and note how they intersect each subsequent triangle in the orbit.

2. Same result here: the fate of the orbit is a single point that is the centroid of the original triangle. Indeed, if you perform this iteration rule with any triangle, you find the same result.

3. The orbit of this iteration rule tends to the famous fractal known as the Koch curve that will be introduced in Lesson 4.

One difficulty in drawing this orbit arises as students try to decide which way to bump out the added triangle. One way to address this difficulty is to formulate the rule: As you traverse the previous image from left to right, always bump out to the left. We will discuss this process at length later.

As with the Sierpiński triangle and the Cantor set, this figure is ideal for "counting." How many line segments make up the figure after each iteration? How long is each successive figure? To what image is the resulting orbit tending? The Koch curve is discussed in more detail in Lesson 4: Copies of Copies.

4. **a.** At each stage of the iteration, we add a single circle of the same size to the right of the previous circle. Therefore the orbit is:

A single circle is added at each stage and the resulting figure extends further to the right. The fate of the orbit is an infinitely long string of circles, each of the same size, extending to the right of the original one.

b. This iteration is different. Here we double the size of the previous figure at each stage:

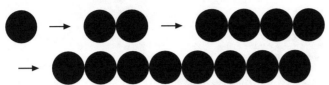

The iteration rule must be read carefully! The fate of the orbit is again an infinitely long string of circles of the same size. So the fate of this orbit is exactly the same as before, even though the number of circles grows much more quickly as we iterate by this rule.

5. The orbit is:

At each stage of the iteration, the two upper points of the original "V" remain tacked down, so the resulting "W," double "W," etc., are always tacked to these same points. This means that more and more line segments appear at each stage—in fact, 2 at the first stage, 4 at the second, 8 at the third, and 2^n at the nth stage. These line segments become ever more closely packed, so after infinitely many iterations the image *fills* a rectangle whose upper two points are the original endpoints on the "V."

This can be quite confusing for everyone. One natural objection is that the outermost segments of the repeated "Ws" never reach the right- or left-hand boundary of the rectangle. This is a valid objection. There is no figure on this orbit that contains these two vertical segments. But we are talking about the "limit" here—a very sophisticated concept at this stage. As we continue to iterate, the figure is getting closer and closer to filling a rectangle.

Incidentally, this orbit is easy to sketch using a paint program that resizes and regroups images.

6. The orbit is:

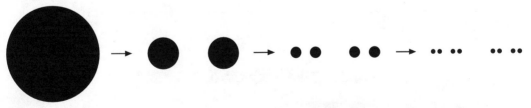

This is exactly the same construction as the Cantor middle-thirds set. If we think of how the circles meet a line segment that forms the horizontal diameter of the original circle, then we see exactly the points in the Cantor set construction. The tops and bottoms of the circles are shrinking toward this diameter, so the only points left after infinitely many iterations lie in the Cantor set.

The same counting arguments that we used for the Cantor set hold here as well.

7. The orbit is:

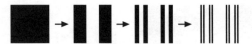

The orbit consists of a collection of rectangles, each of which has the same height as the original rectangle and a smaller and smaller width.

Suppose we look at the bottom of each figure in the orbit. The bottom of each remaining rectangle occupies an interval that produced the Cantor set. Therefore, the fate of the orbit resembles a "hairy" Cantor set with line segments of equal length erected over each point in the set. Alternatively, this could be considered a Cantor "forest," though none of the trees in the forest have branches.

Again, this is an easy construction with a paint program.

LESSON 2 ▷ FRACTALS GENERATED BY REMOVALS

INVESTIGATION 1: THE SIERPIŃSKI CARPET

a.
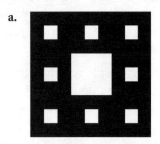

b.

	Original square (the seed)	First iteration	Second iteration	Third iteration	nth iteration in the orbit
Total number of squares remaining	1	8	64	512	8^n
Side length of each square	1	$\frac{1}{3}$	$\frac{1}{9}$	$\frac{1}{27}$	$\left(\frac{1}{3}\right)^n$

INVESTIGATION 2: THE FRACTAL X

a.

b.

	Original square (the seed)	First iteration	Second iteration	Third iteration	nth iteration in the orbit
Total number of squares remaining	1	5	25	125	5^n
Side length of each square	1	$\frac{1}{3}$	$\frac{1}{9}$	$\frac{1}{27}$	$\left(\frac{1}{3}\right)^n$

c. The resulting figure will look rather similar to the Fractal Plus (discussed in this lesson) rotated 45°. It will be a large "X" with increasingly smaller "X" figures off of each branch.

INVESTIGATION 3: THE DIAGONAL

a.

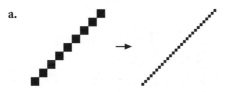

b.

	Original square (the seed)	First iteration	Second iteration	Third iteration	nth iteration in the orbit
Total number of squares remaining	1	3	9	27	3^n
Side length of each square	1	$\frac{1}{3}$	$\frac{1}{9}$	$\frac{1}{27}$	$\left(\frac{1}{3}\right)^n$

c. The resulting figure will be a line segment that is a diagonal of the original square.

d. No, this is not a fractal. In a sense this is a trick question, since we have not yet defined what a fractal is. However, students may agree that whatever a fractal is, it is a more complicated shape than a line segment. So we would accept virtually any similar reason for why this is not a fractal. Indeed, we would even accept the answer: "I don't know what a fractal is, so how can I answer this question?"

INVESTIGATION 4: REMOVING A CORNER

a.

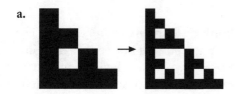

b.

	Original square (the seed)	First iteration	Second iteration	Third iteration	nth iteration in the orbit
Total number of squares remaining	1	3	9	27	3^n
Side length of each square	1	$\frac{1}{2}$	$\frac{1}{4}$	$\frac{1}{8}$	$\left(\frac{1}{2}\right)^n$

c. The outer boundary of this shape will be an isosceles right triangle. The figure will be a Sierpiński right triangle, where all the smaller triangles will be right triangles.

FURTHER EXPLORATION

1. The first three iterations are:

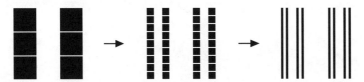

The "final figure" will have infinitely many vertical line segments. If you look at any cross section of the set, you'll see the Cantor middle-thirds set, which you considered in Investigation 6 of Lesson 1. See also Lesson 1, Further Exploration problem 7.

2. Shown below are the seed and the first three iterations.

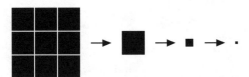

The "final figure" will simply be a point. This point will be the center of the original square.

3. The first three iterations are:

The "final figure" will be infinitely many dots arranged in this square pattern. The blank regions will all look like **+**s. If you look at the bottom line (or top line) in this figure, you will see the Cantor middle-thirds set again. In fact, there are infinitely many horizontal cross sections of this figure that are the Cantor set. Also, the left- and right-hand vertical segments in this figure are the same as the Cantor set, as are other vertical segments.

4. Here is the seed with the first three iterations.

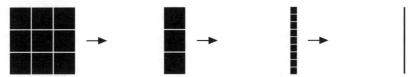

   The "final figure" in this process will be a vertical line segment with the same height as the original square. The line segment would cut the original square in half.

5. To create this fractal, begin with a square. Divide the square into nine equal-sized squares. Then remove the three squares that create the upper right corner.

   The rule:

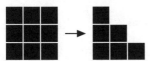

   The first three iterations are:

6. To create the Fractal T, begin with a square. Divide the square into nine equal-sized squares. Remove the lower two corners and the two squares directly above the corners.

   The rule:

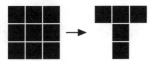

   The first three iterations are:

7. To create the plaid fractal, divide the square into 25 equal-sized squares. Then remove the nine squares that make up the middle cross.

   The iteration rule is:

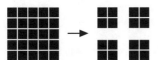

   The first three iterations are:

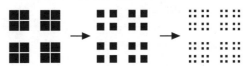

8. Divide the square into nine equal squares. Remove four squares, leaving five squares in a kite shape.

   The rule:

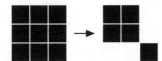

   The first three iterations are:

9. You might name this fractal the Fractal L, or perhaps the FractaLLLLL.

To create this fractal, begin with a square. Divide the square into nine equal squares. Remove the four squares that make up the upper right corner, leaving five squares in an "L" shape.

The iteration rule is:

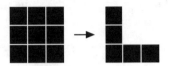

The first three iterations are:

LESSON 3 ▷ SELF-SIMILARITY

INVESTIGATION 1: THE SIERPIŃSKI CARPET

a. To the right is one of the eight self-similar pieces of the Sierpiński carpet that has magnification factor 3.

a. and **b.**

Magnification factor	1	3	9
Number of self-similar pieces	1	8	64

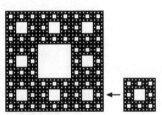

INVESTIGATION 2: THE SIERPIŃSKI HEXAGON

a. To the right is the Sierpiński hexagon with two of the self-similar pieces circled. Each has magnification factor 3.

a. and **b.**

Magnification factor	1	3	9
Number of self-similar pieces	1	6	36

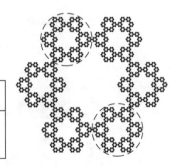

INVESTIGATION 3: THE FRACTAL T

a. To the right is the Fractal T with two of the five self-similar pieces circled. Each has magnification factor 3.

a. and **b.**

Magnification factor	1	3	9
Number of self-similar pieces	1	5	25

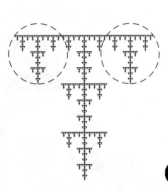

INVESTIGATION 4: A RELATIVE OF THE SIERPIŃSKI TRIANGLE

a. Three of the six self-similar pieces with magnification factor 3 have been circled.

a. and b.

Magnification factor	1	3	9
Number of self-similar pieces	1	6	36

Note that this image differs from the Sierpiński triangle in that the smallest magnification factor is 3, not 2. Also, there are six self-similar pieces in this image with magnification factor 3, whereas the Sierpiński triangle consists of three self-similar pieces with magnification factor 2.

INVESTIGATION 5: THE KOCH CURVE

a. The two middle copies are rotated versions of the whole curve. The first of these has the left endpoint fixed and is rotated by 60° in the counterclockwise direction; the second of these has the right endpoint fixed and is rotated by 60° in the clockwise direction.

a. and b.

Magnification factor	1	3	9
Number of self-similar pieces	1	4	16

INVESTIGATION 6: THE FERN FRACTAL

a. Each of the leaves of the fern is a smaller copy of the entire fern, which has been rotated and/or flipped. The size, and consequently the magnification factor, of each leaf is different—the leaves nearer the base of the stem have a smaller magnification factor than the leaves toward the tip. Additionally, the leaves on the left side of the fern have been rotated about 50° counterclockwise. The leaves on the right side of the fern have been rotated about 50° clockwise and have been flipped (mirror imaged).

Each leaf also contains smaller copies of itself (and the entire fern). Again, looking within each leaf, we find the same varying magnification factor in moving from the base to the tip and the same rotations and flips occurring on the left and right sides.

b. Some examples are mountains, a coastline, trees, root systems of trees, blood vessels in the circulatory system, air passageways of the respiratory system, rivers and their tributaries, yarns or rope made of fibers.

INVESTIGATION 7: THE CANTOR MIDDLE-THIRDS SET

a. The Cantor set consists of a "dust" of points and therefore is difficult to draw. At the fourth stage of the construction, we have a picture like this. (The circled region is explained in b.)

b. The Cantor set consists of 2 pieces each of which has magnification factor 3. Or it consists of 4 pieces with magnification factor 9, or 8 pieces with magnification factor 27, and so forth. The region circled has magnification factor 9.

c. $0, \frac{1}{3}, \frac{1}{9}, \frac{2}{9}, \frac{1}{27}, \frac{2}{27}, \frac{7}{27}, \frac{8}{27}, \frac{1}{81}, \frac{2}{81}, \frac{7}{81}, \frac{8}{81}, \frac{19}{81}, \frac{20}{81}, \frac{25}{81}, \frac{26}{81}$, and so on.

d. $0, 1, \frac{1}{3}, \frac{2}{3}, \frac{1}{9}, \frac{2}{9}, \frac{7}{9}, \frac{8}{9}, \frac{1}{27}, \frac{2}{27}, \frac{7}{27}, \frac{8}{27}, \frac{19}{27}, \frac{20}{27}, \frac{25}{27}, \frac{26}{27}$, and so on.

e. Yes, all of the new numbers lie in the Cantor set. However, not all of them lie in the left-hand side of the Cantor set. For example, $^{19}/_{81}$ lies in the left-hand side of the set, but $3 \cdot {}^{19}/_{81} = {}^{19}/_{27}$ does not lie in the left-hand side of the set.

f. This process will produce other endpoints. Notice that if $^{c}/_{3^n}$ is an endpoint, then $^{c}/_{3^{n-1}}$ is also an endpoint. Similarly, if $^{c}/_{3^n}$ is an endpoint, then $^{c}/_{3^{n+1}}$ is an endpoint.

g. This statement is accurate and is a good description of the self-similarity of the Cantor set. The left-hand portion is a copy of the whole set that has been shrunk down by a factor of 3. Consequently, when you take the left side and magnify it by a factor of 3, you will get back to the original Cantor set. For example, multiplication by 3 leaves 0 unchanged but converts $\frac{1}{3}$ to 1. So multiplication by 3 magnifies the interval between 0 and $\frac{1}{3}$ to the interval from 0 to 1. The middle third of the original interval (between $\frac{1}{9}$ and $\frac{2}{9}$) is magnified by multiplication to the interval from $\frac{1}{3}$ to $\frac{2}{3}$.

h. Magnifying the left portion of the left side of the Cantor set by a factor of 9 produces the entire Cantor set. So multiplying by 9 magnifies this portion of the Cantor set to yield the entire set.

i. The "magnifying glass" relation is $3x - 2$, where x lies in the interval from $\frac{2}{3}$ to 1. For example, if we insert 1 into this expression, we obtain 1; but if we insert $\frac{2}{3}$, we obtain 0. So $3x - 2$ magnifies the interval from $\frac{2}{3}$ to 1 to the entire interval between 0 and 1.

Notice that the desired expression is linear. Using the points $(1, 1)$ and $\left(\frac{2}{3}, 0\right)$, you can determine the equation of the linear function. This magnifying glass magnifies by a factor of 3 (as the other one did) and also translates everything 2 units to the left.

FURTHER EXPLORATION

1. There are an infinite number of self-similar copies of the original image. There are three with a magnification factor of 2, nine with a magnification factor of 4, 27 with a magnification factor of 8, etc. When focusing on any particular copy, the top section is a copy of the entire figure rotated 180°.

2. There are an infinite number of self-similar copies of the original image. There are three with a magnification factor of 2, nine with a magnification factor of 4, 27 with a magnification factor of 8, etc. When focusing on any particular copy, the top section is not rotated; the lower left section is rotated by about 45° in the clockwise direction; the lower right section is rotated by about 45° in the counterclockwise direction.

3. There are an infinite number of self-similar copies of the original image. There are five with a magnification factor of 3, 25 with a magnification factor of 9, 125 with a magnification factor of 27, etc. When focusing on any particular copy, the middle section is rotated by 45° (either direction yields the same figure).

4. There are an infinite number of self-similar copies of the original image. There are five with a magnification factor of 3, 25 with a magnification factor of 9, 125 with a magnification factor of 27, etc. There are no rotations.

5. There are an infinite number of self-similar copies of the original image. There are three with a magnification factor of 2, nine with a magnification factor of 4, 27 with a magnification factor of 8, etc. When focusing on any particular copy, the top portion and lower right portion are not rotated; the lower left section is rotated by 90° counterclockwise.

6. There are an infinite number of self-similar copies of the original image. There are three with a magnification factor of 2, nine with a magnification factor of 4, 27 with a magnification factor of 8, etc. This one's a "toughie" because all of the pieces are rotated. When focusing on one particular copy, each of the 3 pieces of the copy are the original (shrunk down by a factor of 2) rotated 90° clockwise.

LESSON 4 ▷ COPIES OF COPIES

INVESTIGATION 1: TRIPLICATING A SQUARE

a. Here are the next three iterations. (The students only need to create the first two.)

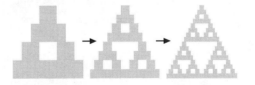

b. The Sierpiński triangle will result if you continue to iterate using this rule.

INVESTIGATION 2: TRIPLICATING WITH A TWIST

a. Here are the next four figures in the orbit. (The students only need to create the first figure.)

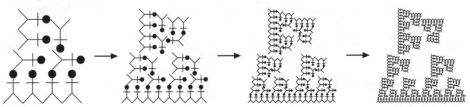

b. This fractal can be thought of as the Sierpiński triangle with the top section rotated. The resulting picture is a fractal that appears several times in Lesson 3: Self-Similarity. See, for example, Transparency 3B.

INVESTIGATION 3: DROP THE PERPENDICULAR

a. The next four figures in this orbit are pictured here. (Students need only draw the next three.)

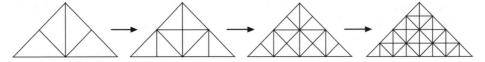

b. When this rule is iterated, the figures will tend toward a 45°-45°-90° triangle that is completely filled in.

INVESTIGATION 4: A SIERPIŃSKI SURPRISE

a. Below are the next four figures in the orbit. (Students are only asked to draw the first one.) Note that although each of the two lower equilateral triangles are traced twice, the direction arrows are the same for both "tracings." Were this not the case, things would get very messy!

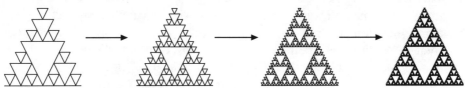

b. The shape is actually approaching the Sierpiński triangle. This too can be confusing because it appears that the sides of the Sierpiński triangle are missing at each stage. That's not quite the case, since the vertices are present at each stage. As we see from the last figure drawn, these vertices are getting closer and closer to filling the sides, and in the limit, they do!

INVESTIGATION 5: PARALLEL SEGMENTS

a. Here are the next four iterations. (Students are only asked to draw the first two.)

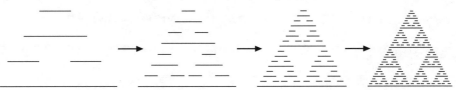

b. As in the previous investigation, the shapes approach the Sierpiński triangle.

Investigation 6: The hat curve

a. Here are the next three figures in the orbit. (Students need only draw the first two.)

b. The resulting fractal will look like figure i on page 61.

Investigation 7: Animating the Koch curve in a flip book

a. Students should draw the first three iterations using their sample *a*-value.

b. The sixth iteration of various *a*-values are shown at right. Of course, students will need software to produce images at this detail.

c. At right is a representative sample of one possible sequence of pages of the flip book. This flip book is short, using only five different frames from five different values of *a*.

Further Exploration

1. a. Here are the next four iterations. (Students were asked to draw three.)

b. The resulting fractal will be figure (ii).

2. a. Here is the generator:

b. Make four copies. Reduce each copy until it fits on a segment of the previous image. The copies will need to be slightly different sizes, because the segments of the generator are not all congruent. Then replace each segment of the previous image with the reduced copy of the generator. Make sure all the hats are pointing up and out.

3. a. Here is the generator:

b. Make four copies. Reduce each copy until it fits on a segment of the previous image. The copies will need to be different sizes, because the segments of the generator are not all congruent. Then replace each segment of the previous image with the reduced copy of the generator. Make sure all the hats are pointing up and out.

4. **a, b,** and **c.** Here is the generator and the next three figures on the orbit. This is a tricky one! To generate the first iteration, make five copies reduced by $\frac{1}{3}$. Replace each segment with one of these copies. Make sure all the hats are pointing up and out.

5. The resulting fractal is the Cantor middle-thirds set, shown here:

    ·· ··   ·· ··   ·· ··   ·· ··   ·· ··   ·· ··   ·· ··   ·· ··

6. The resulting fractal is the Sierpiński hexagon, shown here:

7. **a.** The Koch snowflake is shown here:

    b. The Koch snowflake has infinite perimeter but encloses finite area! This means you could have enough paint to paint the interior but never enough to paint the edge.

8. This example shows a silly face as the original picture, but students can pick any image as their seed. No matter what the initial image, the Sierpiński triangle results.

LESSON 5 ▷ RANDOM ITERATION: THE CHAOS GAME

INVESTIGATION 1: PLAYING THE GAME

a, b, and **c.** It may take quite a while for the pattern to emerge. With only nine points plotted, no clear pattern can be discerned. With groups pooling their data on the overhead, a pattern should become partially clear. Be wary of errors. If one group is off, the Sierpiński triangle may be obscured. Also, an error at some point in the process will throw things off temporarily. With enough iterations, however, eventually the Sierpiński triangle should emerge no matter what.

d. Students skilled at using the graphing calculator can program the calculator to do this process of moving halfway to a randomly selected vertex step by step so that they can see the Sierpiński triangle slowly emerge. Also, several graphing calculator guidebooks contain the instructions for this particular program because of its popularity.

If you use the applet located on the Web site

http://math.bu.edu/DYSYS/applets/fractalina.html

be sure to click clear after each trial. You may also move the three given vertices around by clicking and dragging them. Be careful, however. If you do not click directly on the vertex, the computer will think that you are trying to magnify a portion of the picture. If this is the case, click the zoom button to return to the original picture. Detailed instructions are available at the Web site. If you have trouble getting the applet to work, see the suggestions in the Technology section of the Teacher Notes for this lesson.

INVESTIGATION 2: PLAYING THE GAME WITH THE SIERPIŃSKI TRIANGLE SHOWING

a. Rolling a 1 or 2 moves you halfway toward the *upper* vertex. Rolling a 3 or 4 moves you from this point halfway to the *lower left* vertex, and rolling a 5 or 6 moves you from z_2 halfway to the *lower right* vertex. Note that z_0 is in the largest white triangle; z_1 is in the largest white triangle of the *upper* copy; z_2 is in the largest white triangle of the upper copy of the *lower left* copy; z_3 is in the largest white triangle of the upper copy of the lower left copy of the *lower right* copy.

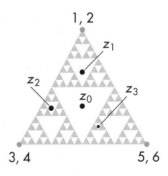

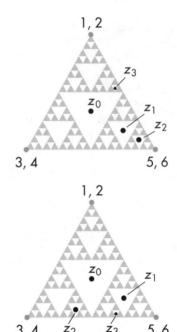

b. Roll 6, 6, 1 (or equivalent). Note that the point z_3 is in the lower right triangle of the lower right triangle of the upper triangle. Alternatively, to locate z_3, focus on the upper triangle (with magnification factor of 2), and move to the lower right triangle of the upper triangle (which has a magnification factor of 4 with the original triangle). Then move to the lower right triangle of the lower right triangle of the upper triangle (which has a magnification factor of 8 with the original triangle).

c. Roll 5, 3, 5 (or equivalent). The point z_3 is located in the lower right triangle of the lower left triangle of the lower right triangle. Alternatively, to find z_3, go to the lower right triangle (which has a magnification factor of 2 with the original triangle); within that, move to the lower left triangle (magnification factor of 4); and within that triangle, move to the lower right triangle (magnification factor of 8).

INVESTIGATION 3: TARGET PRACTICE

a. Die rolls: 1, 3 (or 2, 3; or 1, 4; etc.)

Notice that the shaded region is in the upper triangle of the lower left triangle of the original. Therefore, to get into this region, move toward vertex 1, 2 (the upper vertex) and then toward vertex 3, 4 (the lower left vertex).

b. Die rolls: 5, 3

Notice that the shaded region is in the lower right triangle of the lower left triangle of the original. Therefore, to get into this region, move toward vertex 5, 6 (the lower right vertex) and then toward vertex 3, 4 (the lower left vertex).

c. Die rolls: 1, 3, 1

Notice that the shaded region is in the upper triangle of the lower left triangle of the upper triangle of the original. Therefore, to get into this region, move toward vertex 1, 2 (the upper vertex), then vertex 3, 4 (the lower left vertex), and finally vertex 1, 2 (the upper vertex).

Notice also how this problem is related to Investigation 2.

d. Die rolls: 1, 3, 5

The shaded region is in the upper triangle of the lower left triangle of the lower right triangle of the original. Therefore, to get into this region, the moves need to be toward the upper vertex (1, 2), then the lower left vertex (3, 4) and then the lower right vertex (5, 6).

Notice also how this problem is related to Investigation 2a (it is the same).

INVESTIGATION 4: NONRANDOM CHAOS GAMES

a. The orbit tends toward cycling between two points, both located on the left side of the large triangle. One point is one-third of the distance between vertex 1, 2 and vertex 3, 4 and the other point is two-thirds of the distance between vertex 1, 2 and vertex 3, 4.

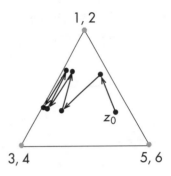

b. The orbit tends toward cycling between two points on the right side of the triangle located one-third and two-thirds of the way between 1, 2 and 5, 6.

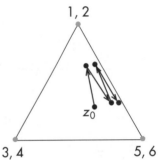

c. The orbit eventually cycles between three points. You can start to see this cycle in the image at the right:

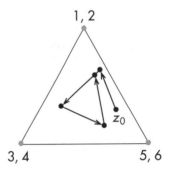

INVESTIGATION 5: ANOTHER CHAOS GAME

a. H ———•—————•——————————•—•——— T
    0 x_2 x_1 x_3 x_0 1

b. H ——————————•—•——————————•—•—•—— T
    0   x_3 x_1 $x_4 x_2$ x_0 1

c. $x_1 = \frac{1}{6} = \left(\frac{1}{3} \cdot \frac{1}{2}\right)$

$x_2 = \frac{1}{18} = \left(\frac{1}{3} \cdot \frac{1}{6}\right)$

$x_3 = \frac{37}{54} = \left[1 - \frac{1}{3}\left(1 - \frac{1}{18}\right)\right]$

d. $x_1 = \frac{3}{4}$

$x_2 = \frac{1}{4}$

$x_3 = \frac{3}{4}$

$x_4 = \frac{1}{4} \ldots$

e. $x_{new} = \left(\frac{1}{3}\right)x$

f. $x_{new} = 1 - \left(\frac{1}{3}\right)(1 - x)$, which simplifies to $x_{new} = \frac{2}{3} + \left(\frac{1}{3}\right)x$.

g. Possible locations for two rolls:

HT (first heads, then tails): $\frac{2}{3} \leq x \leq \frac{7}{9}$ HH: $0 \leq x \leq \frac{1}{9}$

TH: $\frac{2}{9} \leq x \leq \frac{1}{3}$ TT: $\frac{8}{9} \leq x \leq 1$

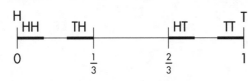

h. The possible combinations of 3 coin flips are HHH, HTH, THH, TTH, HHT, HTT, THT, TTT. The possible positions corresponding to these are as follows:

HHH: $0 \leq x \leq \frac{1}{27}$ HHT: $\frac{2}{3} \leq x \leq \frac{19}{27}$

HTH: $\frac{2}{27} \leq x \leq \frac{1}{9}$ HTT: $\frac{20}{27} \leq x \leq \frac{7}{9}$

THH: $\frac{2}{9} \leq x \leq \frac{7}{27}$ THT: $\frac{8}{9} \leq x \leq \frac{25}{27}$

TTH: $\frac{8}{27} \leq x \leq \frac{1}{3}$ TTT: $\frac{26}{27} \leq x \leq 1$

i. The Cantor middle-thirds set.

FURTHER EXPLORATION

1. Answers may vary. See the Explanation pages for material that helps answer this question.

2. It isn't necessary to choose a seed inside the triangle. The orbit of a seed outside the triangle will also be attracted to the Sierpiński triangle. Have students try this with technology if possible.

3. You will still get a Sierpiński-like triangle. The result will be a Sierpiński triangle skewed to the side. All of the triangles, and the triangles within the triangles, will be right triangles.

4. **a.** Rolls: **2, 4, 5, 3, 1**. The first two moves could be either 2, 4 or 4, 2. The purpose is to get the point somewhere into the interior of a triangle. The next three moves correspond to lower right, lower left, and upper vertices since the target is the lower right triangle of the lower left triangle of the upper triangle of the original.

b. Rolls: **4, 6, 1, 5, 3**. Alternatively: **6, 4, 1, 5, 3**.

5. **a.** The formula for moving the point (x, y) half the distance to the point $(2, 3)$ is:

$$x_{new} = \left(\frac{1}{2}\right)(x + 2)$$

$$y_{new} = \left(\frac{1}{2}\right)(y + 3)$$

b. To change the preceding formula to move a point at the position (x, y) half the distance to the point with coordinates (a, b), replace the 2 and 3 in the formula above with a and b, respectively.

$$x_{new} = \left(\frac{1}{2}\right)(x + a)$$

$$y_{new} = \left(\frac{1}{2}\right)(x + b)$$

You can think of the above two equations as "averaging" equations.

6. We don't want to give away the strategy yet but will give a hint: If you describe the location of the shaded region, you are also describing most of the strategy. See the answer to Lesson 12: Further Exploration problem 3 for a complete analysis of this strategy.

7. Answers will vary depending on the technology available and the game the student chooses to simulate. As mentioned in the Teacher Notes, several graphing calculator guidebooks contain the program steps for the first chaos game.

LESSON 6 ▷ OTHER CHAOS GAMES

INVESTIGATION 1: SIX VERTICES AND A COMPRESSION FACTOR OF 3

a. Rolling 1, 5, 2, 4 in succession yields the figure below.

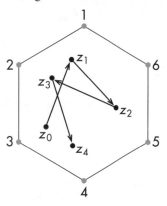

b. Answers will vary.

c. Playing the chaos game with these rules yields an infinite number of self-similar pieces: 6 with a compression factor of 3; 36 with a compression factor of 9; 216 with a compression factor of 27; etc. This is the Sierpiński hexagon pictured below.

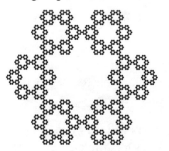

INVESTIGATION 2: THREE VERTICES AND THREE DIFFERENT COMPRESSION FACTORS

a. This image is not easy to draw! But we can give a rough sketch. There is a different compression ratio for each vertex, so you should expect that although the structure will be the same at each vertex, the sizes of the pieces at each vertex will be different. Here's a first attempt at locating the points. You know that each point of the fractal will lie in one of the triangles shown in the diagram.

This second diagram is a little more accurate. Each point of the fractal will lie in one of these triangles.

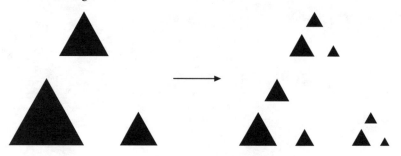

b. After infinitely many iterations you'll see a figure resembling this one:

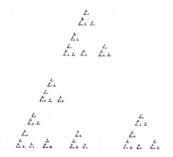

There are infinitely many self-similar pieces. The lower left portion is a self-similar copy with a compression factor of 2; the upper portion has a compression factor of 3; and the lower right portion has a compression factor of 4. Within each of these copies, there are more self-similar copies. In the lower left portion are self-similar copies with compression factors of $4\,(2 \cdot 2)$, $6\,(2 \cdot 3)$, and $8\,(2 \cdot 4)$ with the whole figure. Likewise, the lower right portion has within it self-similar copies with compression factors of 8, 12, and 16. There are also self-similar copies with compression factors of 9, 24, and 81 to name a few. (Notice, however, that there are no copies with compression factors of 10, 25, and 82. Do you know why? Which factors are possible and which are not?)

Technology Tip: To play this chaos game with Fractalina, use the following setup:

Vertex	Rotation	Comp factor	x coord	y coord
A	0	2	−50	−50
B	0	3	50	−50
C	0	4	0	36.6

A is the lower left vertex, B is the top vertex, and C is the lower right vertex. The exact x- and y-coordinates can vary as long as the three vertices are those of an equilateral triangle.

INVESTIGATION 3: FIVE VERTICES AND A COMPRESSION FACTOR OF 2.5

a. Answers will vary.

b. Based on the location and the number of vertices, you should expect to see a figure that has 5 self-similar copies with compression factor of 2.5; 25 self-similar copies with compression factor of 6.25; etc. If the compression factor were 2, each of the smaller self-similar copies would overlap its neighbors. With a compression factor of 2.5, however, a gap will be left between corresponding sides of the copies. Since $1/2.5 = 0.4$, if you let the length of the side of the original pentagon be 1 unit, each of the 5 "largest" self-similar copies will extend for 0.4 units along one of the original sides; the gap between the copies will have length 0.2, as shown in the diagram. Note that the small pentagons have a small overlap. You may change the compression factor to 2.7 to eliminate these overlaps.

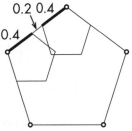

The result of playing this chaos game is pictured at right. Note that, because of the overlaps described before, there are also some small overlaps in this image.

Again, you may find it helpful to use Fractalina to see the resulting attractor. Though it is fairly easy to estimate coordinates for the vertices of a regular pentagon, finding those points exactly might prove to be an interesting challenge.

INVESTIGATION 4: COMPRESSION FACTOR 2 ON THE CORNERS OF A SQUARE

a. You should expect to find 4 smaller copies of the square (one at each vertex) with compression factor of 2; 16 copies of the square with compression factor of 4 (with the entire picture); 64 with compression factor of 8; etc.

b. What you actually find is a solid square!

c. Initially, this result does seem a little surprising, since the figure doesn't seem to display any self-similarity.

d. Looking more closely, you actually do find 4 smaller copies of the square with compression factor of 2; 16 copies of the square with compression factor of 4; etc. Notice that each of these four smaller copies has $\frac{1}{4}$ the area of the original square (the dimensions are $\frac{1}{2}$ those of the original square). With a total of four of them, the entire original square is covered by the copies! Similarly, each of the 16 copies has an area equal to $\frac{1}{16}$ the area of the original square. Again, these copies cover the entirety of the original square.

e. To find a fractal image using these vertices, we must choose a compression factor larger than 2. This will yield a fractal image such as the one shown here.

INVESTIGATION 5: USING JUST TWO VERTICES

a. Answers will vary. You should expect a line segment extending between the two vertices. Using the same analysis as in Investigation 4, there will be two copies of the entire figure with compression factor of 2; four copies with compression factor of 4; etc. Again, the smaller copies cover the original segment completely.

Note also that even if the seed does not lie between the two vertices, the attractor will still be the line segment. (Recall that the first few points in the orbit are always erased.)

b. If the compression factor is 3 rather than 2, then the result is the Cantor middle-thirds set!

INVESTIGATION 6: DESCRIBE THE GAME

a. There are five vertices, as shown in the diagram. The compression factor at each vertex is 3.

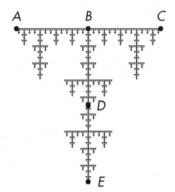

b. There are eight vertices, as shown in the diagram. The compression factor at each vertex is 3.

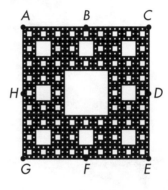

INVESTIGATION 7: TARGET PRACTICE

a.

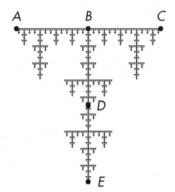

b. The sequence A, B, A is one solution. Another is B, B, A. The sequence can be done in a minimum of three moves, and it must end with the two moves B and then A. The initial move of A or B brings the point into the interior of the main square. Then B, A moves the point into the interior of the target.

c. A, C, D, B is one solution. The other is B, C, D, B. The minimum number of moves is four, and the sequence must end with the three moves C, D, B. Notice that the moves C, C, D, B or D, C, D, B put you on the boundary of the target, not in its interior.

d. The sequence has a minimum of four moves and must end with the three moves A, A, C. So the two solutions are A, A, A, C and B, A, A, C. Notice that if the sequence A, A, C is done without the first move, then you end up on the boundary of the desired square instead of in the interior.

FURTHER EXPLORATION

1. **a.** This figure has five vertices and a compression factor of 3 at each vertex.

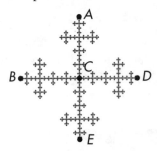

b. This figure has four vertices and a compression factor of 3. This is an example of a Sierpiński square rotated (or a Sierpiński diamond).

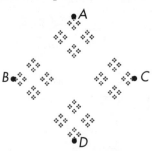

c. This figure has six vertices and a compression factor of 3 at each vertex.

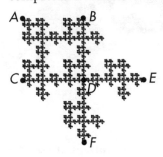

d. This figure has four vertices. The compression factor is not the same at each vertex. The upper two vertices (A and B) have a compression factor of 3, and the lower two vertices (C and D) have a compression factor of 2.

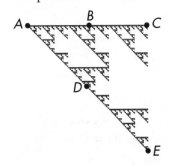

e. This figure has five vertices and a compression factor of 3.

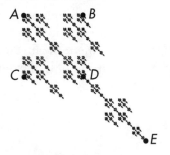

f. This figure also has five vertices and a compression factor of 3. Though the number of vertices, the compression factor and four of the five vertices are identical to those in (e), notice how different the resulting fractal is! The placement of each vertex is critical.

g. This figure has eight vertices, each with a compression factor of approximately 4.

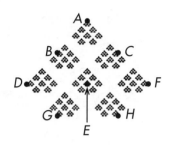

2. Vertex 1 is at $(0, 1)$. To determine this, recall that each interior angle in a regular hexagon measures 120°; when bisected by a line through the opposite vertex, two angles of 60° are produced. This fact gives the measures of angles 1 and 2 of the triangle that is drawn. Since the sum of the angles of a triangle is 180°, the third angle must also measure 60°. So the triangle is an equilateral triangle. Since the measure of each side of the hexagon is 1, the measure of each side of the triangle is 1. Therefore, vertex 1 is located at the point $(0, 1)$.

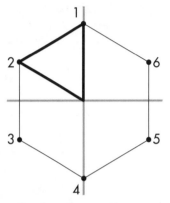

With this knowledge, we can now figure out the coordinates for the other vertices.

vertex 2: $\left(-\frac{\sqrt{3}}{2}, \frac{1}{2}\right)$ 　　vertex 3: $\left(-\frac{\sqrt{3}}{2}, -\frac{1}{2}\right)$ 　　vertex 4: $(0, -1)$

vertex 5: $\left(\frac{\sqrt{3}}{2}, -\frac{1}{2}\right)$ 　　vertex 6: $\left(\frac{\sqrt{3}}{2}, \frac{1}{2}\right)$

To find these, first focus on vertex 2. Its y-coordinate must be $\frac{1}{2}$ since it is half of one of the sides of the hexagon. Using the Pythagorean theorem on the right triangle shown in the diagram, you can find that the length of the other side of the triangle is $\sqrt{3}/2$. Since the x-coordinate for vertex 2 is negative, its coordinate position is $\left(-\sqrt{3}/2, \frac{1}{2}\right)$. From here, use the symmetric properties of the diagram to determine the other vertices.

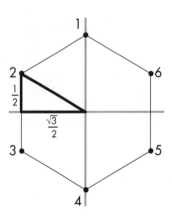

3. The formulas to move ⅔ of the distance toward any of the six vertices are as follows:

Vertex	Coordinates	Formulas	
		x-value	y-value
1	$(0, 1)$	$x_1 = \frac{1}{3}x_0$	$y_1 = \frac{2}{3} + \frac{1}{3}y_0$
2	$\left(-\frac{\sqrt{3}}{2}, \frac{1}{2}\right)$	$x_1 = -\frac{\sqrt{3}}{3} + \frac{1}{3}x_0$	$y_1 = \frac{1}{3} + \frac{1}{3}y_0$
3	$\left(-\frac{\sqrt{3}}{2}, -\frac{1}{2}\right)$	$x_1 = -\frac{\sqrt{3}}{3} + \frac{1}{3}x_0$	$y_1 = -\frac{1}{3} + \frac{1}{3}y_0$
4	$(0, -1)$	$x_1 = \frac{1}{3}x_0$	$y_1 = -\frac{2}{3} + \frac{1}{3}y_0$
5	$\left(\frac{\sqrt{3}}{2}, -\frac{1}{2}\right)$	$x_1 = \frac{\sqrt{3}}{3} + \frac{1}{3}x_0$	$y_1 = -\frac{1}{3} + \frac{1}{3}y_0$
6	$\left(\frac{\sqrt{3}}{2}, \frac{1}{2}\right)$	$x_1 = \frac{\sqrt{3}}{3} + \frac{1}{3}x_0$	$y_1 = \frac{1}{3} + \frac{1}{3}y_0$

4. Answers will vary depending on the programming language students use.

LESSON 7 ▷ ROTATIONS AND THE CHAOS GAME

INVESTIGATION 1: THE TOP VERTEX WITH A TWIST

a. First move halfway to the top vertex and then rotate 90° clockwise. Next move halfway to vertex 5, 6. And once again, move halfway to vertex 5, 6.

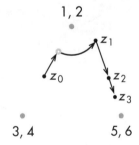

b. First move halfway to the top vertex and then rotate 90° clockwise. Next, again move halfway to the top vertex and rotate 90° clockwise. Finally move halfway to vertex 3, 4.

c. First move halfway to the top vertex and then rotate 90° clockwise. Next, again move halfway to the top vertex and rotate 90° clockwise. Iterate on this two more times.

Notice that z_0, z_2, z_4, and the vertex are collinear, as are z_1, z_3, and the vertex.

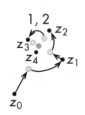

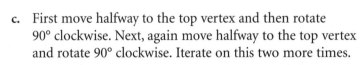

d. The result will be fractal image B. Note that the circled region (see diagram) is the entire figure compressed by a factor of 2 and then rotated 90° clockwise. Fractal images A and C don't have this characteristic.

e. The fractal in A was generated in the same way as the fractal in B except that the rotation for the top vertex is 90° counterclockwise instead of 90° clockwise. The location of the vertices and the compression factors remain the same. (This fractal was explained in the Explanation pages.)

The fractal in C was generated with the same vertices and rules for the bottom two vertices as were used for the fractals in A and B. The top vertex still has a compression factor of 2, but there is a different rotation. The rotation appears to be about 30° counterclockwise. To determine this, estimate by inspection (or use trigonometry or your knowledge of special right triangles) the measure of any one of the angles shown in the diagram. (There are other angles with the same measure—infinitely many, in fact! Only three have been shown.) The vertices have also been drawn in the diagram.

INVESTIGATION 2: BOTTOM VERTICES GET A TWIST

a. The fractal pictured in C is generated by this chaos game. Notice that the circled figure on the left is the entire figure compressed by a factor of 2 and then rotated 45° clockwise. Similarly, the circled portion on the right is the entire figure compressed by a factor of 2 and then rotated 45° counterclockwise. The top region has no rotation.

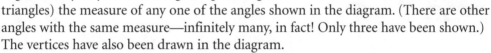

b. The fractal in A is generated with the three vertices of an equilateral triangle, each with a compression factor of 2. The lower left vertex also has a rotation of approximately 45° counterclockwise; the lower right vertex has a rotation of approximately 45° clockwise; there is no rotation for the top vertex. (Notice that some of the self-similar copies overlap in this fractal.)

As were the fractals in A and C, fractal B is generated with the three vertices of an equilateral triangle, each with a compression factor of 2. The lower left vertex has a rotation of approximately 15° counterclockwise; the lower right vertex has a rotation of approximately 15° clockwise; the upper vertex has no rotation.

INVESTIGATION 3: THE KOCH CURVE

It may be easiest to experiment using the web-based applet Fractalina. The locations of the four vertices are shown in the diagram at right.

Once the vertices have been found experimentally, take careful note of their locations, as this can give you a clue for finding vertices of other fractals: vertex *A* is located in the left copy of the left copy of the left copy of the ...; similarly, vertex *D* is located in the right copy of the right copy of the right copy of the .... Vertices *B* and *C* may seem a little more challenging, but the same process can be applied. If you think about "the second copy" as the self-similar copy that is rotated 60° counterclockwise, vertex *B* is located in the second copy of the second copy of the second copy of the .... Vertex *C* can be found in the same way.

INVESTIGATION 4: DESCRIBE THE GAME

For each of the following fractals, the vertices have been shown on the diagram and the rotation and compression values that would be used to generate the fractals using the web-based applet Fractalina have been given. Note that there are many options for the *x*- and *y*-coordinates; it's the relative positioning that is important. For the values of the rotations, angle measures between −180° and 180° have been given. An angle such as −90° could be written in other ways, however (e.g., 270° or −450°).

a.

Vertex	Rotation	Comp factor	x coord	y coord
A	0°	3	−150	150
B	0°	3	150	150
C	45°	3	0	0
D	0°	3	−150	−150
E	0°	3	150	−150

Other angles (such as −45°) could be used at the central vertex.

b. The top piece of this figure has been rotated; the other two have not been rotated.

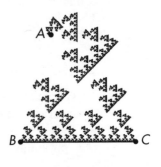

Vertex	Rotation	Comp factor	x coord	y coord
A	45°	2	−40	120
B	0°	2	−150	−150
C	0°	2	150	−150

FRACTALS: A TOOL KIT OF DYNAMICS ACTIVITIES
©1999 KEY CURRICULUM PRESS

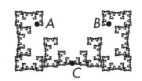

c. As always, the exact position of these vertices is not too important; it is the relative scale that matters. Students can get more or less the same image with a variety of different vertex locations.

Vertex	Rotation	Comp factor	x coord	y coord
A	−90°	2	−80	80
B	90°	2	80	80
C	0°	2	0	−20

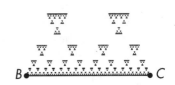

d. This is similar to the Sierpiński triangle, except the top vertex features a 180° rotation and a compression factor of 3, not 2.

Vertex	Rotation	Comp factor	x coord	y coord
A	180°	3	0	75
B	0°	2	−150	−150
C	0°	2	150	−150

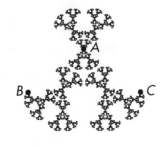

e. This fractal has three self-similar copies, each with compression factor of 2. The top copy has been rotated by 180°. The other two copies have rotations of 30° and −30°, respectively.

Vertex	Rotation	Comp factor	x coord	y coord
A	180°	2	0	50
B	−30°	2	−100	−30
C	30°	2	100	−30

f. Students may find many different coordinates to produce this image.

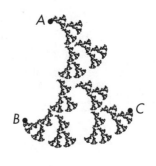

Vertex	Rotation	Comp factor	x coord	y coord
A	25°	2	−25	125
B	−25°	2	−125	−75
C	25°	2	125	−75

INVESTIGATION 5: MOVIES

Each picture has three vertices located on the vertices of an equilateral triangle. In all the frames, the rule for the bottom two vertices is "compress by a factor of 2." For the upper vertex, the compression factor is also 2, but a rotation is involved (except in the first frame). The sixth frame looks very similar to an old friend and has a rotation of about 90°; the tenth figure has a rotation of 180°. Notice that there is a total of 19 diagrams, where the first and last look identical; so in 18 steps, the successive rotations of the top vertex take it all the way around. That is, 18 steps were taken to rotate 360°; consequently, the rotation of the top vertex in each frame is 20° greater (in the counterclockwise direction) than in the previous frame. (Someone might argue that the last frame exhibits no rotation. This could be true, but based on the pattern of the 17 previous frames, a rotation of 360° makes more sense.)

To create the motion, the degree of rotation was slowly increased, perhaps a degree at a time, and then the figures were displayed rapidly in succession.

Technology tip: Students can make movies like this one by using the Java applet "Franimate" at **http://math.bu.edu/DYSYS/applets**.

FURTHER EXPLORATION

1. For each of the following fractals, the vertices have been shown on the diagram and the values that would be used to generate the fractals using Fractalina have been given. Note that there are many options for the x- and y-coordinates; it's the relative positioning that is important. For the values of the rotations, the angle between −180° and 180° has been given. An angle such as −90° could be written in other ways, however (e.g., 270° or −450°).

    a.

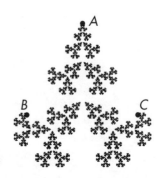

Vertex	Rotation	Comp factor	x coord	y coord
A	0°	2	0	100
B	−45°	2	−75	−30
C	45°	2	75	−30

b. The three self-similar copies have been circled in the diagram. Notice all three copies are the original figure upside down.

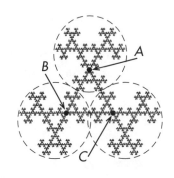

Vertex	Rotation	Comp factor	x coord	y coord
A	180°	2	0	30
B	180°	2	−20	−5
C	180°	2	20	−5

c. This fractal can be tricky. At first, there may appear to be six smaller copies. However, these six copies aren't scaled-down replicas of the originals. The figure is like a double kite, and there are three copies of this figure, two of which have been circled.

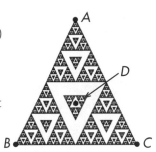

Vertex	Rotation	Comp factor	x coord	y coord
A	0°	2	0	0
B	−90°	2	45	90
C	−90°	2	−45	−90

d. This is similar to the Sierpiński triangle, but notice that the middle region (which is blank in the Sierpiński triangle) has a small copy of the entire figure (turned upside down) within it. Because there are four self-similar copies of the triangle, there are going to be four vertices. The central vertex will have a compression factor that is larger than that of the other vertices and will also have a rotation of 180°.

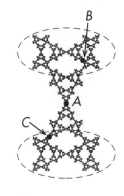

Vertex	Rotation	Comp factor	x coord	y coord
A	0°	2	0	75
B	0°	2	−75	−75
C	0°	2	75	−75
D	180°	5	0	−25

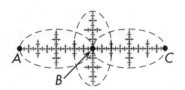

e. This fractal has three self-similar copies, each with compression factor of 2. The "middle" copy has been rotated and the copies overlap, making it difficult to distinguish the three. As it is symmetric, vertex B can have a rotation of 90° or −90°. Vertex B is at the center of the figure.

Vertex	Rotation	Comp factor	x coord	y coord
A	0°	2	−75	0
B	90°	2	0	0
C	0°	2	75	0

f. It may be helpful to think of this figure as "figure (d) with no gaps." To get no gaps, use the same four vertices as in figure (d), keep the rotation, but change the compression factor of vertex D (the central vertex) to 2.

Vertex	Rotation	Comp factor	x coord	y coord
A	0°	2	0	75
B	0°	2	−75	−75
C	0°	2	75	−75
D	180°	2	0	−25

Another way to create this figure is to have more than four vertices so that the self-similar copies overlap (if the compression factor is low enough) and thereby fill in the space. Experiment and see what you come up with!

2. **a.** The results from the Further Exploration problem 3 in Lesson 6 give you the following transformations:

$$\text{for } (0, 0): \quad x_1 = \tfrac{1}{3}x_0, \quad y_1 = \tfrac{1}{3}y_0$$

$$\text{for } (1, 0): \quad x_1 = \tfrac{2}{3} + \tfrac{1}{3}x_0, \quad y_1 = \tfrac{1}{3}y_0$$

So the question is: what are the other two vertices? We see that C must be $\frac{1}{3}$ and F must be 0 and $A = \frac{1}{6}$ and $D = \frac{\sqrt{3}}{6}$.

b. To find B and E, we need to know where one other point will get mapped. More specifically, it must be a point for which the y-coordinate is not 0. Notice that the vertex of the generator gets mapped to the "tip" of the rotated copy of the curve. See the diagram.

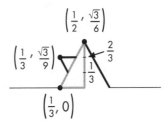

this point, $\left(\frac{1}{2}, \frac{\sqrt{3}}{6}\right)$, gets mapped to

this point,

(0, 0) $\left(\frac{1}{3}, 0\right)$ (1, 0)

So if we can determine the coordinates to which the point $\left(\frac{1}{2}, \frac{\sqrt{3}}{6}\right)$ gets mapped, we'll be able to find B and E. Note that the point is directly over the point $\left(\frac{1}{3}, 0\right)$. The point is also $\frac{2}{3}$ of the way between 0 and $\frac{\sqrt{3}}{6}$. To prove this more rigorously, use similar triangles. This is a very good (and fairly difficult) review of the properties of similar triangles!

By substituting $\left(\frac{1}{2}, \frac{\sqrt{3}}{6}\right)$ for $\left(x_0, y_0\right)$ and $\left(\frac{1}{3}, \frac{\sqrt{3}}{9}\right)$ for $\left(x_1, y_1\right)$ and solving the equations:

$$x_1 = \frac{1}{6}x_0 + By_0 + \frac{1}{3}$$

$$y_1 = \frac{\sqrt{3}}{6}x_0 + Ey_0 + 0$$

you can solve for the missing coefficients. Solving, we find that $B = -\frac{\sqrt{3}}{6}$ and $E = \frac{1}{6}$.

c. Solve the system of equations

$$x_0 = \frac{1}{6}x_0 - \frac{\sqrt{3}}{6}y_0 + \frac{1}{3}$$

$$y_0 = \frac{\sqrt{3}}{6}x_0 + \frac{1}{6}y_0$$

The result is $x_0 = \frac{5}{14}$ and $y_0 = \frac{\sqrt{3}}{14}$ so the fixed point is $\left(\frac{5}{14}, \frac{\sqrt{3}}{14}\right)$.

d. Answers will vary depending on the programming language.

LESSON 8 ▷ INVESTIGATING SIERPIŃSKI

INVESTIGATION 1: THE WORLD'S LARGEST SIERPIŃSKI TRIANGLE!

a. You need nine copies to produce a triangle with a 40-centimeter base. (You need three copies of the 20-centimeter-base triangle, each of which is made up of three copies of the original triangle.)

b. For 80 centimeters, you need 27 copies.

c. For 160 centimeters, 81 copies.

d. 59,049 copies will make a triangle with a base measure of 102.4 meters!

INVESTIGATION 2: PASCAL'S TRIANGLE

a. It's the Sierpiński triangle again!

You may have first shaded all the circles on the two outer sides, recognizing that these would all be 1's. You may have recognized that the triangular shape with three shaded circles is a unit that repeats over and over. The first two rows make up such a unit. In the top four rows there are three such units, which together create another triangle!

b. If the two circles above are both unshaded or both shaded, the circle below will be unshaded. If one of the above circles is shaded and one unshaded, then the circle below will be shaded.

c. Note that if you add two even numbers or two odd numbers together, the result is an even number. If you add an odd number and an even number (in either order of course), the result is an odd number. Shaded circles are the odd numbers and unshaded circles are the even numbers.

INVESTIGATION 3: SHADING DIFFERENT CIRCLES

The structure is self-similar. Though it resembles the Sierpiński triangle, there are significant differences. The key unit in this figure is a triangle of six shaded circles. The top three rows make up such a unit. Six groups of these triangular units (six shaded circles each) then make up the next larger triangle. (An example of this is what we see in the top nine rows.) We would need six of these triangles to construct the next larger triangle. The figure only has enough rows to show three of these six.

We haven't seen this exact fractal before. It can be generated using six vertices located at the vertices and midpoints of the sides of an equilateral triangle. Each vertex would have a compression factor of 3. It could also be generated by removals using an equilateral triangle as the seed and the following rule: Divide the triangle into nine triangles of the same size and then remove three, as shown in the diagram at right.

INVESTIGATION 4: CELLULAR AUTOMATA

a. Notice that the rule "if a pair of circles are both unshaded or both shaded, then the lower circle is unshaded" is equivalent to the fact that the sum of either two even numbers or two odd numbers is an even number. The rule "if one of the upper circles is shaded and the other unshaded, then the lower circle is shaded" is equivalent to the fact that the sum of an odd number and an even number is an odd number.

b. It's the Sierpiński triangle once again.

INVESTIGATION 5: FRACTALS IN 3-D—THE SIERPIŃSKI TETRAHEDRON

Stage number	0	1	2	3	4	n
Number of tetrahedra	1	4	16	64	256	4^n
Volume of each tetrahedron (cubic units)	1	$\frac{1}{8}$	$\frac{1}{64}$	$\frac{1}{512}$	$\frac{1}{4096}$	$\frac{1}{8^n}$
Total volume (cubic units)	1	$\frac{1}{2}$	$\frac{1}{4}$	$\frac{1}{8}$	$\frac{1}{16}$	$\frac{1}{2^n}$

INVESTIGATION 6: BUILD YOUR OWN SIERPIŃSKI TETRAHEDRON

a. 6 toothpicks

b. 4 marshmallows

c. 2

d. 3 more—one for each vertex of its bottom triangle

e. 6

f. At the first stage of the construction you need 10 marshmallows $(16 - 6)$

g. 24

h. marshmallows: $34 = (4 \cdot 10 - 6)$
toothpicks: $96 = (4 \cdot 24)$

   i.   marshmallows: 130   **j.**   marshmallows: 514
       toothpicks: 384   toothpicks: 1536

   k.   marshmallows: 4 times the number in   **l.** $6 + 6 \cdot 4 + 6 \cdot 4^2 + 6 \cdot 4^3 + \ldots$
       the previous stage, minus 6; $+ 6 \cdot 4^{n-1}$
       toothpicks: four times the number in
       the previous stage (or $6 \cdot 4^n$)

   m. It all depends upon what n is.   **n.** $10 \cdot 2^n$ centimeters

INVESTIGATION 7: UNDERSTANDING THE SIERPIŃSKI TETRAHEDRON

   a. After one iteration   **b.** Yes. The bottom face looks the same.
       each face looks
       like the first stage   **c.**
       of the construction
       of the Sierpiński
       triangle.

   d. After iterating infinitely often, we find a Sierpiński triangle on each face.

   e. The solid being removed has eight faces. Four of the
       faces are the "removed" triangles, one from each face
       of the original tetrahedron. The other four faces are
       on "the inside"; each is one of the faces of the four
       tetrahedra created by the removal. (One face is the
       bottom side of the top tetrahedron; a second face is

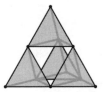

       the front face of the back tetrahedron; etc.) To better "see" the figure that is removed,
       we'll take the picture of the tetrahedron in the first stage and delete the four smaller
       tetrahedra. It appears that an octahedron is left.

INVESTIGATION 8: THE SIERPIŃSKI HEXAGON

   a. By dividing the hexagon into six equilateral triangles,
       we can see that each interior angle of the hexagon will
       have measure 120°.

   b. You can determine the height of each equilateral
       triangle by using the Pythagorean theorem or your
       knowledge of 30°-60°-90° triangles. The height of
       one such triangle is $\sqrt{3}/2$. Double this to get the height
       of the hexagon: $\sqrt{3}$, or about 1.732.

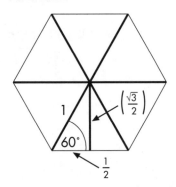

   c. The area of each equilateral triangle is $\left(\frac{1}{2}\right)bh$, which is
       $\sqrt{3}/4$. Multiply this by 6 to get the area of the hexagon:
       $3\sqrt{3}/2$, or about 2.598.

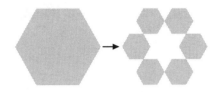

d. At the first stage, we compress the hexagon by a factor of 3.

e. Each side of the six smaller hexagons has length $\frac{1}{3}$ unit.

f. The area of each is $\frac{1}{9}$ that of the larger hexagon, or $\sqrt{3}/6$.

g. Recall that this is the first stage in the construction of the Koch snowflake curve.

h. The next figure is shown at right.

i. At this stage, there are 36 smaller hexagons.

j. The central removed region looks a bit like a six-pointed star with extra spikes.

k. After infinitely many iterations, in the middle of the figure we find the Koch snowflake! Each side of the snowflake is the famous Koch curve.

LESSON 9 ▷ FRACTAL DIMENSION

INVESTIGATION 1: FAMOUS FRACTALS

a.

i. 3 self-similar pieces

ii. Each has a magnification factor of 2.

iii. The fractal dimension is $(\log 3)/(\log 2) \approx 1.585$.

You could look at the 9 self-similar pieces, each with a magnification factor of 4. This would yield fractal dimension $(\log 9)/(\log 4)$. The result of $(\log 9)/(\log 4)$ is also 1.585, since

$$\frac{\log 9}{\log 4} = \frac{\log 3^2}{\log 2^2} = \frac{2\log 3}{2\log 2} = \frac{\log 3}{\log 2}$$

There are other options as well. Regardless of the size of the pieces you use, the fractal dimension will not vary. For each of the fractals below, only one of the options has been given.

b.

i. 2 self-similar pieces

ii. Each has a magnification factor of 3.

iii. The fractal dimension is $(\log 2)/(\log 3) \approx 0.6309$.

c.

i. 4 self-similar pieces

ii. Each has a magnification factor of 3.

iii. The fractal dimension is $^{(\log 4)}/_{(\log 3)} \approx 1.262$.

d.

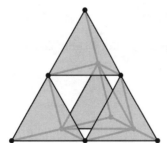

i. 4 self-similar pieces

ii. Each has a magnification factor of 2.

iii. The fractal dimension is $^{(\log 4)}/_{(\log 2)} = {}^{(2\log 2)}/_{(\log 2)} = 2$.

INVESTIGATION 2: ORDERING FRACTALS BY DIMENSION

Answers to part (i) will vary. Answers to parts (ii) and (iii) are given below.

a. $\dim = \dfrac{\log 3}{\log 2} \approx 1.585;\ 4$ **b.** $\dim = \dfrac{\log 6}{\log 3} \approx 1.63;\ 5$ or 6

c. $\dim = \dfrac{\log 8}{\log 3} \approx 1.89;\ 8$ **d.** $\dim = \dfrac{\log 5}{\log 3} \approx 1.46;\ 2$

e. $\dim = \dfrac{\log 6}{\log 3} \approx 1.63;\ 5$ or 6 **f.** $\dim = \dfrac{\log 8}{\log 4} \approx 1.5;\ 3$

g. $\dim = \dfrac{\log 4}{\log 3} \approx 1.26;\ 1$ **h.** $\dim = \dfrac{\log 7}{\log 3} \approx 1.77;\ 7$

The fractal in **e.** has the same dimension as the fractal in **b.** Written from lowest to highest fractal dimension, the letters corresponding to the fractals are g, d, f, a, b & e, h, c.

INVESTIGATION 3: TOPOLOGICAL DIMENSION

a. `.. ..   .. ..        .. ..   .. ..                    .. ..   .. ..         .. ..   .. ..`

The Cantor middle-thirds set has topological dimension 0 since any point can be surrounded in the plane by a small circle that does not meet the Cantor set.

b. The topological dimension of the Sierpiński tetrahedron is 1. This is because you can surround any of its points with arbitrarily small spheres that meet the Sierpiński triangle in a set of dimension 0. More specifically, for the tetrahedron we will always be able to find arbitrarily small spheres that surround a point and that meet the set in only four points, which is a set of dimension 0.

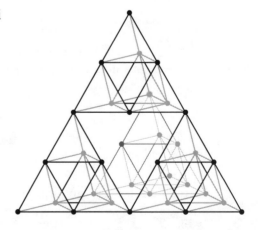

c. The Sierpiński hexagon, like the Sierpiński triangle, has a topological dimension of 1. This is because we can always thread small circles through the vertices of the figure so that the circles meet the set in exactly two points. We can do this for any point in the set. We can also make these circles arbitrarily small.

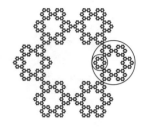

INVESTIGATION 4: THE MENGER SPONGE

a. To generate the Menger sponge, start with a cube and divide it into 27 cubes. Remove the cube at the core and remove the middle cube of each face. This will be a total of 7 cubes removed. Iterate this process. The result will be the Menger sponge.

A second method is to compress the cube by a factor of 3, copy the compressed cube 20 times, and then assemble the copies in the shape of the original cube such that no copy is in the middle of the structure or the middle of a face.

b. The fractal dimension is therefore:

$$d = \frac{\log 20}{\log 3} = 2.73$$

c. Each face of this figure is a Sierpiński carpet.

INVESTIGATION 5: THE CANTOR MIDDLE-FIFTHS SET

a.

```
———————        ———————        ———————   ———————
0                        2        3               1
                        ─        ─
                        5        5
```

The intervals remaining after the second stage of construction are:

$0 \le x \le 0.16$; $0 \le x \le \frac{4}{25}$;

$0.24 \le x \le 0.4$; $\frac{6}{25} \le x \le \frac{2}{5}$;

$\qquad\qquad$ or

$0.6 \le x \le 0.76$; $\frac{3}{5} \le x \le \frac{19}{25}$;

and $0.84 \le x \le 1$.   and $\frac{21}{25} \le x \le 1$.

b. And at the following stage:

```
——  ——      ——  ——        ——   ↑        ——  ——
0  8         6      2         3           87         1
  ───       ──     ─         ─          ───
  125       25     5         5          125
```

$0 \le x \le \frac{8}{125}$ $\frac{3}{5} \le x \le \frac{83}{125}$

$\frac{12}{125} \le x \le \frac{4}{25}$ $\frac{87}{125} \le x \le \frac{19}{25}$

$\frac{6}{25} \le x \le \frac{38}{125}$ $\frac{21}{25} \le x \le \frac{113}{125}$

$\frac{42}{125} \le x \le \frac{2}{5}$ $\frac{117}{125} \le x \le 1$

c. At the nth stage of this process, there are 2^n intervals.

d. Each piece has magnification factor 2.5^n.

e. The fractal dimension is $(\log 2)/(\log 2.5) \approx 0.756$.

f. The fractal dimension of this set is larger than the Cantor middle-thirds set, which has a fractal dimension of about 0.6309. This makes sense because in the middle-fifths fractal you remove less of the line segment at each stage than in the middle-thirds fractal $\left(\frac{1}{5} \text{ as opposed to } \frac{1}{3}\right)$. Therefore we might expect that the middle-fifths fractal would be fuller or denser.

FURTHER EXPLORATION

1. Following the process of construction used to make the Cantor middle-thirds and middle-fifths sets, you can create a fractal with any dimension between 0 and 1. Suppose that the intended dimension is d. You would want to solve the equation $(\log 2)/(\log m) = d$ for m, where m is the magnification factor. The "2" in the numerator represents the number of self-similar pieces of the Cantor set after magnification m. Using base 10 logarithms, you find

$$\frac{\log 2}{d} = \log m$$

$$10^{(\log 2)/d} = m$$

$$2^{1/d} = m$$

Since we want $d \leq 1$, we have $m \geq 2$. When $d = 1$, we have $m = 2$. As d tends to 0, m gets very large. Suppose, for example, you wanted to construct a Cantor set fractal of dimension 0.8. To find your magnification factor, solve for m.

$$2^{(1/0.8)} = m$$

$$2.38 \approx m$$

To create the fractal, take a segment, duplicate it, then compress both segments by $\frac{1}{2.38}$. Arrange the shorter segments so they replace the original segment. Iterate this process on each smaller segment to continue building the Cantor set with fractal dimension 0.8.

2. The fractal dimension of the object is:

$$\frac{\log 4}{\log\left(\frac{1}{A}\right)}$$

When $A = \frac{1}{4}$, the object would just be the original line segment and would have fractal dimension $(\log 4)/(\log 4) = 1$.

When A is $\frac{1}{2}$, the generator for the fractal would look like a segment of length 1 with a segment of length $\frac{1}{2}$ perpendicular to it $\left(\text{which is actually made up of two segments of length } \frac{1}{2}\right)$. It is pictured here:

The resulting "fractal" would be a filled-in triangle with the original line segment as its base and the perpendicular segment of the generator as its altitude. The fractal dimension would be $(\log 4)/(\log 2) = 2$.

If you made a movie and each frame of the film was a picture of this object as A increases, you would see the following. Initially, when $A = \frac{1}{4}$, you'd see a line segment. The line segment would bulge up in the middle, slowly getting higher and higher as A increases. The bulge also would get "spikier" as A increases, as would the rest of the fractal. The fractal will seem to get thicker as A increases. The last frame of the movie, when $A = \frac{1}{2}$, would be a filled-in triangle with an altitude equal to half the length of the base. In viewing this movie, you would see fractals of all dimensions ranging from 1 to 2. Three frames of the movie are shown on the first of the Explanation pages in this lesson.

3. To construct a fractal with any given dimension between 1 and 2, we can follow the general method of construction described in the previous solution. Let d be the dimension of the fractal you're trying to construct. For these Koch-like curves, the dimension is $d = (\log 4)/(\log (1/A))$, where $1/A$ is the magnification factor m. The "4" in the numerator represents the four self-similar pieces of the set found at magnification m. Solving the preceding equation for A yields $A = 4^{-1/d}$. When $d = 1$, we see that $A = \frac{1}{4}$. When $d = 2$, we find $A = \frac{1}{2}$.

4. The dimension of the Sierpiński hexagon is $(\log 6)/(\log 3) \approx 1.63$. (The Sierpiński hexagon is fractal (b) of Investigation 2.) One fractal of the same dimension is the fractal pictured in (e) of Investigation 2. A second is the figure at right that resembles the Sierpiński triangle.

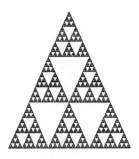

At right is a third fractal of the same dimension.

A final fractal is the one that would be generated using the method given in the solution to problem 2, using an A value found as follows:

$$A = 4^{-\log 3/\log 6} \approx \frac{1}{2.34} \text{ or } 0.427$$

There are many other fractals with this dimension.

LESSON 10 ▷ NATURAL FRACTALS

GENERAL COMMENTS

The answers given for this lesson are just examples of possible solutions. The exact data may be somewhat different from what you obtain in your experiments. Nevertheless, the slope of the line through the data points—and, consequently, the resulting fractal dimension— should be in the general ballpark of the value given.

To measure the fractals, a compass can be useful. Fix the opening of the compass to match the length of the ruler being used, and then step along the fractal by turning the compass. (This works best if you have a very sharp pencil in the compass as well as a sharp pivot point.) To minimize error, you may want to run two or three trials with the same ruler and then average the results.

Students may find it helpful to use a graphing calculator or a spreadsheet program that will let them enter the data, take the logarithms, plot the data, and compute the slope of the line of best fit.

These solutions were done using a spreadsheet program. The slopes were calculated from the data. The lines shown in the graph are approximations to the best fit line.

INVESTIGATION 1: CUMULUS CLOUD

a. Answers will vary.

b.

Ruler length	Number of rulers
1	1
$\frac{1}{2}$	2.75
$\frac{1}{4}$	6.4
$\frac{1}{8}$	12.5

c.

log (Length)	log (Number)
0	0
-0.30	0.439
-0.60	0.806
-0.90	1.097

d.

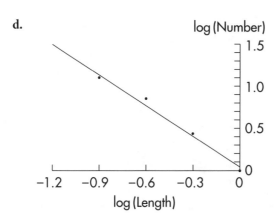

e. The dimension of this fractal is about 1.22 since the slope of the line through these data points is approximately −1.22.

INVESTIGATION 2: MORE FRACTALS

a. A lightning bolt

Ruler length	Number of rulers
1	1
0.5	2.85
0.25	6.85
0.125	14.5

log (Length)	log (Number)
0	0
−0.30	0.455
−0.60	0.836
−0.90	1.16

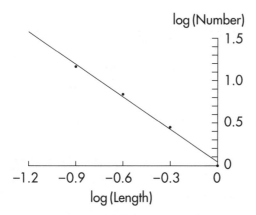

The slope of the best-fit line is −1.28. Therefore the fractal has a dimension of 1.28.

b. Koch-like curve

Ruler length	Number of rulers
1	1
0.5	2.25
0.25	8.25
0.125	32

log (Length)	log (Number)
0	0
−0.30	0.352
−0.60	0.916
−0.90	1.51

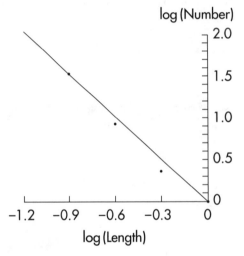

The fractal dimension of this fractal is about 1.69.

c. Another cloud

Ruler length	Number of rulers
1	1
0.5	2.4
0.25	4.9
0.125	10.3

log (Length)	log (Number)
0	0
−0.30	0.380
−0.60	0.690
−0.90	1.01

FRACTALS: A TOOL KIT OF DYNAMICS ACTIVITIES

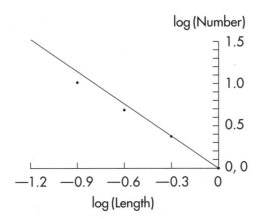

The fractal dimension of this object is about 1.11.

INVESTIGATION 3: A NEW RULER

Using rulers of size $\frac{1}{2^n}$ changes the values you get for the data but does not change the slope of the line through the data on a log-log plot. The fractal dimension is the same (at least approximately), regardless of the length of the measuring tool.

FURTHER EXPLORATION

For the following two exercises, the "1-unit ruler" used to generate the data was 10 cm long. Again, remember that because of inaccuracies in these measurements, you may obtain somewhat different results.

1. Maine

Ruler length	Number of rulers
1	1.3
$\frac{1}{2}$	2.3
$\frac{1}{4}$	5.5
$\frac{1}{8}$	16.7
$\frac{1}{16}$	37.5

log (Length)	log (Number)
$\log(1) = 0$	0.114
$\log\left(\frac{1}{2}\right) = -0.30$	0.362
$\log\left(\frac{1}{4}\right) = -0.60$	0.740
$\log\left(\frac{1}{8}\right) = -0.90$	1.22
$\log\left(\frac{1}{16}\right) = -1.2$	1.57

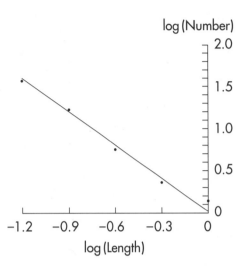

The fractal dimension of this section of the coastline of Maine is about 1.26.

2. Massachusetts

Ruler length	Number of rulers
1	1.6
$\frac{1}{2}$	2.9
$\frac{1}{4}$	8.3
$\frac{1}{8}$	20.5
$\frac{1}{16}$	45

log (Length)	log (Number)
$\log(1) = 0$	0.204
$\log\left(\frac{1}{2}\right) = -0.30$	0.462
$\log\left(\frac{1}{4}\right) = -0.60$	0.919
$\log\left(\frac{1}{8}\right) = -0.90$	1.312
$\log\left(\frac{1}{16}\right) = -1.2$	1.65

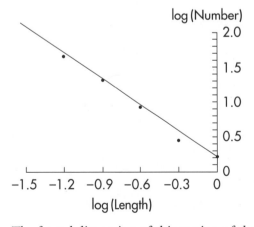

The fractal dimension of this section of the Massachusetts coastline is about 1.24.

FRACTALS: A TOOL KIT OF DYNAMICS ACTIVITIES

©1999 KEY CURRICULUM PRESS

LESSON 11 ▷ AREAS AND PERIMETERS OF FRACTALS

INVESTIGATION 1: SUM SOME SERIES

a. $= \dfrac{1}{1 - \frac{1}{3}} = \dfrac{3}{2}$

b. $= \dfrac{1}{1 - \frac{2}{5}} = \dfrac{5}{3}$

c. There is no finite sum for this expression. It gets infinitely large. Notice the ratio is greater than 1.

d. $= 3$. The series is 1 less than the series

$$1 + \frac{3}{4} + \left(\frac{3}{4}\right)^2 + \left(\frac{3}{4}\right)^3 + \left(\frac{3}{4}\right)^4 + \cdots = \dfrac{1}{1 - \frac{3}{4}} = 4$$

so the sum is 3.

e. $= \dfrac{1}{1 - \left(\frac{1}{3}\right)^2} = \dfrac{1}{1 - \frac{1}{9}} = \dfrac{9}{8}$

f. $= 2$. To sum, separate the 1 and factor out a 2 from the expression:

$$1 + 2\left(\frac{1}{3} + \frac{1}{3^2} + \frac{1}{3^3} + \ldots\right).$$

The sum within parentheses is 1 less than the sum in part (a), or $\frac{3}{2} - 1 = \frac{1}{2}$. So, the sum is $1 + (2)\left(\frac{1}{2}\right) = 2$.

INVESTIGATION 2: THE AREA UNDER THE KOCH CURVE

$$A\left(1 + \frac{4}{9} + \left(\frac{4}{9}\right)^2 + \left(\frac{4}{9}\right)^3 + \left(\frac{4}{9}\right)^4 + \ldots\right) = A\left(\dfrac{1}{1 - \frac{4}{9}}\right) = \frac{9}{5}A$$

INVESTIGATION 3: THE LENGTH OF THE KOCH CURVE

a. 17 stages. The length of the Koch curve at stage n is $\left(\frac{4}{3}\right)^n$. The requirement is that the curve is longer than 100 units. Therefore, solve $\left(\frac{4}{3}\right)^n > 100$ for the smallest value of n that will make the statement true. $\left(\frac{4}{3}\right)^{16} \approx 99.8$, so it is in the 17th stage that the length of 100 units is first exceeded.

b. 19 stages. Use the same argument as above. (Notice how quickly the length is growing at these later stages! It doesn't take long to double the length.)

INVESTIGATION 4: AREA OF THE SIERPIŃSKI TRIANGLE

a.

Stage	Number of triangles removed	Image	Area of each triangle removed	Total area removed at this stage	Total area removed so far
0	0		none	none	none
1	1		$\frac{1}{4}$	$\frac{1}{4}$	$\frac{1}{4}$
2	3		$\frac{1}{16} = \left(\frac{1}{4}\right)^2$	$3\left(\frac{1}{4}\right)^2$	$\frac{1}{4} + 3\left(\frac{1}{4}\right)^2$
3	$9 = 3^2$		$\frac{1}{64} = \left(\frac{1}{4}\right)^3$	$3^2\left(\frac{1}{4}\right)^3 = \frac{9}{64}$	$\frac{1}{4} + 3\left(\frac{1}{4}\right)^2 + 3^2\left(\frac{1}{4}\right)^3$
4	$27 = 3^3$		$\frac{1}{256} = \left(\frac{1}{4}\right)^4$	$3^3\left(\frac{1}{4}\right)^4 = \frac{27}{256}$	$\frac{1}{4} + 3\left(\frac{1}{4}\right)^2 + 3^2\left(\frac{1}{4}\right)^3 + 3^3\left(\frac{1}{4}\right)^4$
n	3^{n-1}		$\left(\frac{1}{4}\right)^n$	$3^{n-1}\left(\frac{1}{4}\right)^n$	$\frac{1}{4} + 3\left(\frac{1}{4}\right)^2 + 3^2\left(\frac{1}{4}\right)^3 + \cdots$ $+ 3^{n-1}\left(\frac{1}{4}\right)^n$

b. The Sierpiński triangle has area 0 because the removed areas sum to 1 (the area of the original triangle), as shown by the following geometric series:

$$\frac{1}{4} + 3\left(\frac{1}{4}\right)^2 + 3^2\left(\frac{1}{4}\right)^3 + \cdots = \frac{1}{4}\left(1 + \frac{3}{4} + \left(\frac{3}{4}\right)^2 + \left(\frac{3}{4}\right)^3 + \cdots\right) = \frac{1}{4}\left(\frac{1}{1 - \frac{3}{4}}\right) = \frac{1}{4}(4) = 1.$$

Students may ask how something with zero area can still be visible and still be made of infinitely many points. Remind them that a line has zero area but is made of infinitely many points and is visible——at least the way we represent a line.

INVESTIGATION 5: PERIMETER OF THE SIERPIŃSKI TRIANGLE

a.

Stage	Number of triangles removed	Image	Area of each triangle removed	Total area removed at this stage	Total area removed so far
0	none		none	none	$3S$
1	3		$\frac{S}{2}$	$3\frac{S}{2}$	$3S + \frac{3S}{2}$
2	$9 = 3^2$		$\frac{S}{4} = \frac{S}{2^2}$	$9\frac{S}{4} = 3^2\left(\frac{S}{2^2}\right)$	$3S + \frac{3S}{2} + \frac{9S}{4}$
3	$27 = 3^3$		$\frac{S}{8} = \frac{S}{2^3}$	$27\frac{S}{8} = 3^3\left(\frac{S}{2^3}\right)$	$3S + \frac{3S}{2} + \frac{9S}{4} + \frac{27S}{8}$
4	$81 = 3^4$		$\frac{S}{16} = \frac{S}{2^4}$	$81\frac{S}{16} = 3^4\left(\frac{S}{2^4}\right)$	$3S + \frac{3S}{2} + \frac{9S}{4} + \frac{27S}{8} + \frac{81S}{16}$
n	3^n		$\frac{S}{2^n}$	$3^n\left(\frac{S}{2^n}\right)$	$3S + \frac{3S}{2} + \frac{9S}{4} + \frac{27S}{8} + \cdots$ $+ \left(\frac{3}{2}\right)^n S$

b. The perimeter is getting larger and larger without bound. Since the ratio of the geometric sequence for the "total length added so far" is $\frac{3}{2}$ (which is greater than 1), the sum keeps increasing as you take larger and larger values of n.

FURTHER EXPLORATION

1. Here is a table for the Cantor middle-thirds set.

Stage	Number of segments removed	Length of each segment removed	Total length removed at this stage	Total length removed so far
0	0	none	none	none
1	1	$\frac{1}{3}$	$\frac{1}{3}$	$\frac{1}{3}$
2	2	$\frac{1}{9} = \frac{1}{3^2}$	$\frac{2}{9}$	$\frac{1}{3} + \frac{2}{9}$
3	$4 = 2^2$	$\frac{1}{27} = \frac{1}{3^3}$	$\frac{4}{27}$	$\frac{1}{3} + \frac{2}{9} + \frac{4}{27}$
n	2^{n-1}	$\frac{1}{3^n}$	$\frac{2^{n-1}}{3^n}$	$\frac{1}{3} + \frac{2}{9} + \frac{4}{27} + \cdots + \frac{2^{n-1}}{3^n} =$ $\frac{1}{3}\left[1 + \frac{2}{3} + \left(\frac{2}{3}\right)^2 + \cdots + \left(\frac{2}{3}\right)^{n-1}\right]$

Since the length removed equals

$$\frac{1}{3}\left[1 + \frac{2}{3} + \left(\frac{2}{3}\right)^2 + \cdots\right] = \frac{1}{3}\left(\frac{1}{1 - \frac{2}{3}}\right) = \left(\frac{1}{3}\right)(3) = 1$$

the Cantor middle-thirds set has length 0.

2. Recall that to create the Sierpiński carpet, you divide the square into nine equal-sized squares and remove the middle one $\left(\text{having } \frac{1}{9} \text{ of the area of the original}\right)$.

Stage	Number of squares removed	Area of each square removed	Total area removed at this stage	Total area removed so far
0	0	none	none	none
1	1	$\frac{1}{9}$	$\frac{1}{9}$	$\frac{1}{9}$
2	8	$\frac{1}{81} = \left(\frac{1}{9}\right)^2$	$8\left(\frac{1}{9}\right)^2$	$\frac{1}{9} + 8\left(\frac{1}{9}\right)^2$
3	$64 = 8^2$	$\frac{1}{729} = \left(\frac{1}{9}\right)^3$	$8^2\left(\frac{1}{9}\right)^3 = \frac{64}{729}$	$\frac{1}{9} + 8\left(\frac{1}{9}\right)^2 + 8^2\left(\frac{1}{9}\right)^3$
4	8^3	$\left(\frac{1}{9}\right)^4$	$8^3\left(\frac{1}{9}\right)^4$	$\frac{1}{9} + 8\left(\frac{1}{9}\right)^2 + 8^2\left(\frac{1}{9}\right)^3 + 8^3\left(\frac{1}{9}\right)^4$
n	8^{n-1}	$\left(\frac{1}{9}\right)^n$	$8^{n-1}\left(\frac{1}{9}\right)^n$	$\frac{1}{9} + 8\left(\frac{1}{9}\right)^2 + 8^2\left(\frac{1}{9}\right)^3 + \cdots + 8^{n-1}\left(\frac{1}{9}\right)^n$

The sum of the area removed is

$$\frac{1}{9}\left[1 + \frac{8}{9} + \left(\frac{8}{9}\right)^2 + \left(\frac{8}{9}\right)^3 + \cdots\right] = \frac{1}{9}\left(\frac{1}{1 - \frac{8}{9}}\right) = 1.$$

Since all of the original square's area is removed, the area of the Sierpiński carpet is 0. So it is has the same area as the Sierpiński triangle.

3. This fractal is similar to the Koch snowflake curve but with different lengths for the segments of the generator.

Suppose that the area under the triangle of the generator is A units. In the next stage, each triangle added will have an area $\left(\frac{2}{5}\right)^2 A$ or $\frac{4A}{25}$.

Stage	Number of triangles	Area of each triangle	Total area
0	0	0	0
1	1	A	A
2	4	$\frac{4A}{25}$	$A + 4\left(\frac{4}{25}\right)A = A + \frac{16}{25}A$
3	$16 = 4^2$	$\left(\frac{4}{25}\right)^2 A$	$A + 4\left(\frac{4}{25}\right)A + 4^2\left(\frac{4}{25}\right)^2 A = A + \left(\frac{16}{25}\right)A + \left(\frac{16}{25}\right)^2 A$
4	$64 = 4^3$	$\left(\frac{4}{25}\right)^3 A$	$A + \left(\frac{16}{25}\right)A + \left(\frac{16}{25}\right)^2 A + \left(\frac{16}{25}\right)^3 A$
n	4^{n-1}	$\left(\frac{4}{25}\right)^{n-1} A$	$A + \left(\frac{16}{25}\right)A + \left(\frac{16}{25}\right)^2 A + \cdots + \left(\frac{16}{25}\right)^{n-1} A$

As n gets infinitely large, the sum of the area under the curve is

$$A\left[1 + \left(\frac{16}{25}\right) + \left(\frac{16}{25}\right)^2 + \cdots\right] = A\left(\frac{1}{1 - \frac{16}{25}}\right) = \frac{25}{9}A.$$

4. To solve this, think about the length removed at each stage. In the first stage, there will be one segment of length $\frac{1}{5}$ removed; each remaining segment will have length $\frac{2}{5}$. So, at the second stage, the removed segments each have length $\frac{1}{5} \cdot \frac{2}{5} = \frac{2}{25}$. Since we remove two of them, the length removed at this stage is $\frac{4}{25}$. The remaining segments now have length $\frac{4}{25}$, so at the third stage, four segments of length $\frac{4}{125}$ are removed, giving removed area $\frac{4^2}{5^3}$. At the nth stage, there will be 2^{n-1} segments of length $\frac{2^{n-1}}{5^n}$. So we remove $\frac{4^{n-1}}{5^n}$ at this stage.

Therefore, the total length removed can be computed by finding the sum:

$$\frac{1}{5} + \frac{4}{5^2} + \frac{4^2}{5^3} + \ldots = \frac{1}{5}\left(1 + \frac{4}{5} + \frac{4^2}{5^2} + \frac{4^3}{5^3} + \ldots\right) = \frac{1}{5}\left(\frac{1}{1 - \frac{4}{5}}\right) = 1$$

5. Recall that to construct the Sierpiński tetrahedron, you copy the original tetrahedron four times, reduce the dimensions of each by a factor of 2, and then reassemble. Since each copy is reduced by a factor of 2, the volume is $\frac{1}{2} \cdot \frac{1}{2} \cdot \frac{1}{2} = \frac{1}{8}$ the original tetrahedron. Therefore, with four copies, you have $\frac{1}{2} = \left(\frac{1}{8}\right) \cdot 4$ the volume you had originally. This is repeated at each stage of construction, so each time you have $\frac{1}{2}$ the volume you had before. More precisely, at stage n, the volume is $\frac{1}{2^n}$ the volume of the original tetrahedron. As n gets larger and larger, $\frac{1}{2^n}$ tends to 0.

   Copying the original tetrahedron and reducing by a factor of 2 produces a tetrahedron with $\frac{1}{4}$ of the surface area of the original. Since there are four copies made, and $4 \cdot \frac{1}{4} = 1$, the surface area of the tetrahedron does not change. At each stage, the surface area of the Sierpiński tetrahedron will be S. So the Sierpiński tetrahedron has finite surface area (equal to S) but 0 volume.

6. Recall that the Menger sponge was the cube-like object in Investigation 4 of Lesson 9. Each face of the sponge is a Sierpiński carpet. To create the sponge, begin with a cube, divide it into 27 cubes of equal size, and remove seven smaller cubes: one cube from the middle of each face, and the small cube in the center. (This leaves 20 smaller cubes, each having $\frac{1}{27}$ of the volume of the original.)

   Assume that the volume of the original cube is 1.

Stage	Number of cubes removed	Volume of each cube removed	Total volume removed
1	7	$\frac{1}{27}$	$\frac{7}{27}$
2	$7 \cdot 20$	$\left(\frac{1}{27}\right)^2$	$7\left(\frac{1}{27}\right) + 7 \cdot 20\left(\frac{1}{27}\right)^2$
3	$7 \cdot 20^2$	$\left(\frac{1}{27}\right)^3$	$7\left(\frac{1}{27}\right) + 7 \cdot 20\left(\frac{1}{27}\right)^2 + 7 \cdot 20^2\left(\frac{1}{27}\right)^3$
4	$7 \cdot 20^3$	$\left(\frac{1}{27}\right)^4$	$7\left(\frac{1}{27}\right) + 7 \cdot 20\left(\frac{1}{27}\right)^2 + 7 \cdot 20^2\left(\frac{1}{27}\right)^3 + 7 \cdot 20^3\left(\frac{1}{27}\right)^4$
n	$7(20)^{n-1}$	$\left(\frac{1}{27}\right)^n$	$\left(\frac{7}{27}\right)\left[1 + \frac{20}{27} + \left(\frac{20}{27}\right)^2 + \cdots + \left(\frac{20}{27}\right)^{n-1}\right]$

Since the total volume removed is then

$$\frac{7}{27}\left(\frac{1}{1 - {}^{20}\!/\!{}_{27}}\right) = \left(\frac{7}{27}\right)\left(\frac{27}{7}\right) = 1$$

the volume of the Menger sponge is 0.

The surface area of the Menger sponge is infinite, however.

Suppose you start with a surface area of $6S$ square units, meaning that the surface area of each of the six faces is S square units. To construct the sponge, you divide the cube into 27 smaller cubes. Each face of these smaller cubes has an area of ${}^{S}\!/\!{}_{9}$ since there are nine smaller squares per face.

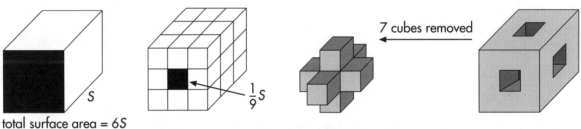

total surface area = $6S$

At stage 1, seven cubes are removed. This removes six of these smaller square faces, each with surface area $\left({}^{1}\!/\!{}_{9}\right)S$ (one from the center of each face), for a total of $\left({}^{6}\!/\!{}_{9}\right)S$. (The seventh one, which is inside, doesn't have an effect on the surface area.) However, there are also new faces added. For each of the six cubes removed, four new smaller square faces are added, each with an area of $\left({}^{1}\!/\!{}_{9}\right)S$. So there is a gain of 24 (i.e., $4 \cdot 6$) smaller squares to the surface area. This is a gain of $\left({}^{24}\!/\!{}_{9}\right)S$.

So, you lose $\left({}^{6}\!/\!{}_{9}\right)S$ and gain $\left({}^{24}\!/\!{}_{9}\right)S$, for a net gain of $\left({}^{18}\!/\!{}_{9}\right)S$, which is $2S$. The surface area increases from $6S$ to $8S$. The surface area is ${}^{4}\!/\!{}_{3}$ times as great as it was.

This removal process is repeated, and at each stage, the object has a surface area ${}^{4}\!/\!{}_{3}$ times as great as the one before. As you iterate, the surface area of the Menger sponge becomes infinitely large.

LESSON 12 ▷ DECODING THE CANTOR SET

INVESTIGATION 1: DECODING THE ENDPOINTS

a. ${}^{1}\!/\!{}_{9}$: LL RRRRRR ... **b.** ${}^{2}\!/\!{}_{9}$: LR LLLLLLL ... **c.** ${}^{7}\!/\!{}_{9}$: RL RRRRRR ...

d. ${}^{8}\!/\!{}_{9}$: RR LLLLLLL ... **e.** ${}^{1}\!/\!{}_{27}$: Code: LLL RRRRRRR ... ${}^{19}\!/\!{}_{27}$: Code: RLL RRRRRR ...

${}^{2}\!/\!{}_{27}$: Code: LLR LLLLLLLL ... ${}^{20}\!/\!{}_{27}$: Code: RLR LLLLLLL ...

${}^{7}\!/\!{}_{27}$: Code: LRL RRRRRRR ... ${}^{25}\!/\!{}_{27}$: Code: RRL RRRRRR ...

${}^{8}\!/\!{}_{27}$: Code: LRR LLLLLLLL ... ${}^{26}\!/\!{}_{27}$: Code: RRR LLLLLLL ...

f. ${}^{20}\!/\!{}_{81}$: Code: LRLR LLLLLL ...   **g.** ${}^{26}\!/\!{}_{81}$: Code: LRRR LLLLLL ...

Shown on the diagram below are the locations of these endpoints. For simplicity, only the left $\frac{1}{3}$ of the Cantor middle-thirds set is shown.

$$0 \qquad\qquad \frac{1}{9} \qquad\qquad \frac{2}{9} \quad \underset{\frac{20}{81}}{\uparrow} \qquad\qquad \underset{\frac{26}{81}}{\uparrow}\frac{1}{3}$$

INVESTIGATION 2: POINTS THAT ARE NOT ENDPOINTS

Answers may vary. Here are three different code names that never repeat:

LR LLRR LLLRRR LLLLRRRR . . .

R L RR LLL RRRRR LLLLLLLL . . . (a Fibonacci Cantor point)

L R LL R LLL R LLLL R LLLLL R LLLLLL R . . .

INVESTIGATION 3: SELF-SIMILARITY

a. Notice that you have already found the code names for eight of the 16 endpoints in Investigation 1, part (e).

1. For the interval $0 \le x \le \frac{1}{27}$ LLL LLLLLLLL . . . represents 0 and LLL RRRRRRRR . . . represents $\frac{1}{27}$.

2. For the interval $\frac{2}{27} \le x \le \frac{1}{9}$ LLR RRRRRRR . . . represents $\frac{1}{9}$ and LLR LLLLLLL . . . represents $\frac{2}{27}$.

3. For the interval $\frac{2}{9} \le x \le \frac{7}{27}$ LRL LLLLLLLL . . . represents $\frac{7}{27}$ and LRL RRRRRRRR . . . represents $\frac{2}{9}$.

4. For the interval $\frac{8}{27} \le x \le \frac{1}{3}$ LRR RRRRRRR . . . represents $\frac{1}{3}$ and LRR LLLLLLL . . . represents $\frac{8}{27}$.

5. For the interval $\frac{2}{3} \le x \le \frac{19}{27}$ RLL LLLLLLLL . . . represents $\frac{2}{3}$ and RLL RRRRRRR . . . represents $\frac{19}{27}$.

6. For the interval $\frac{20}{27} \le x \le \frac{7}{9}$ RLR RRRRRRR . . . represents $\frac{7}{9}$ and RLR LLLLLLL . . . represents $\frac{20}{27}$.

7. For the interval $\frac{8}{9} \le x \le \frac{25}{27}$ RRL LLLLLLLL . . . represents $\frac{8}{9}$ and RRL RRRRRRR . . . represents $\frac{25}{27}$.

8. For the interval $\frac{26}{27} \le x \le 1$ RRR RRRRRRR . . . represents 1 and RRR LLLLLLL . . . represents $\frac{26}{27}$.

b. When looking at the whole Cantor set, it is possible to take the entire set, reduce it by a factor of 3, and then, after duplicating it, place one copy so that its left endpoint is at 0 and the other copy so that its left endpoint is at $\frac{2}{3}$ (and right endpoint at 1). The result is the entire Cantor set once again.

With the L-R sequence notation, we can effectively model this process. Suppose that you had a list of all of the points in the Cantor set, written out in their R-L sequence notation. First, insert a blank space at the beginning of each R-L sequence, recalling that each sequence represents a number. This begins to model reducing by a factor of 3. Next, copy the entire list: with one list, insert an L in each blank space, and with the other, insert an R in each blank space. This is like placing one copy so that it has a left endpoint at 0 and the other copy so that it has a left endpoint at $2/3$. The result is the entire Cantor set once again, as the two lists combined represent every number in the Cantor set. So within each portion of the Cantor set is the entire Cantor set!

INVESTIGATION 4: DECODE THE CODE

Note that you encoded the first three values in Investigation 1.

a. $8/9$, since

$$\frac{2}{3} + \frac{2}{9} + 0 + 0 + \ldots = \frac{8}{9}$$

b. $1/9$, since

$$\frac{0}{3} + \frac{0}{3^2} + \frac{2}{3^3} + \frac{2}{3^4} + \frac{2}{3^5} + \ldots = \frac{2}{3^3}\left(1 + \frac{1}{3} + \frac{1}{3^2} + \frac{1}{3^3} + \ldots\right) = \frac{2}{3^3}\left(\frac{1}{1 - 1/3}\right) = \frac{2}{27}\left(\frac{3}{2}\right) = \frac{1}{9}$$

c. $20/27$, since

$$\frac{2}{3} + \frac{0}{3^2} + \frac{2}{3^3} + 0 + 0 + \ldots = \frac{20}{27}$$

d. $3/4$, since

$$\frac{2}{3} + \frac{0}{3^2} + \frac{2}{3^3} + \frac{0}{3^4} + \frac{2}{3^5} + \ldots = \left(\frac{2}{3} + \frac{2}{3^3} + \frac{2}{3^5} + \frac{2}{3^7} + \cdots\right) =$$

$$\frac{2}{3}\left(1 + \frac{1}{3^2} + \frac{1}{3^4} + \frac{1}{3^6} + \cdots\right) = \frac{2}{3}\left(\frac{1}{1 - (1/3^2)}\right) = \frac{2}{3}\left(\frac{1}{8/9}\right) = \frac{3}{4}$$

e. $9/13$, since

$$\frac{2}{3} + 0 + 0 + \frac{2}{3^4} + 0 + 0 + \frac{2}{3^7} + 0 + 0 + \ldots = \frac{2}{3}\left(1 + \frac{1}{3^3} + \frac{1}{3^6} + \frac{1}{3^9} + \cdots\right) =$$

$$\frac{2}{3}\left(\frac{1}{1 - (1/3^3)}\right) = \frac{2}{3}\left(\frac{1}{26/27}\right) = \frac{2}{3} \cdot \frac{27}{26} = \frac{9}{13}$$

f. $11/12$. The number is equal to $2/3 + 2/9 + 0 + 2/3^4 + 0 + 2/3^6 + 0 + 2/3^8 + \ldots$. Notice that the pattern doesn't really start until the LR sequence repeats. For ease in computing, determine the sum of the LRLRLR . . . sequence and add this value to $2/3 + 2/9$.

The LRLRLR . . . sequence sums to $1/26$, since

$$\left(\frac{2}{3^4} + \frac{2}{3^6} + \frac{2}{3^8} + \cdots\right) = \frac{2}{3^4}\left(1 + \frac{1}{3^2} + \frac{1}{3^4} + \cdots\right) = \frac{2}{3^4}\left(\frac{1}{1 - 1/3^2}\right) = \frac{2}{81}\left(\frac{1}{8/9}\right) = \frac{1}{36}$$

Adding this to $2/3 + 2/9$, we get $11/12$.

INVESTIGATION 5: DECODING THE SIERPIŃSKI TRIANGLE

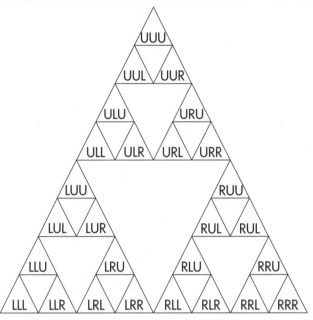

Another way to create this triangle is to make three copies of the triangle at the second stage of construction (pictured in the text), put an L at the beginning of each letter sequence on one of these copies, add an R at the beginning of each letter sequence of the second, and similarly add U's on the third copy. Then appropriately assemble the three copies.

INVESTIGATION 6: DECODING THE VERTICES

a. A = UUUUU . . .

   B = LLLLL . . .

   C = RRRRR . . .

b. A = URRRRR . . . or RUUUUU . . .

   B = LUUUUU . . . or ULLLLL . . .

   C = LRRRRR . . . or RLLLLL . . .

c. A = UURRRRR . . . or URUUUUU . . .

   B = LLUUUUU . . . or LULLLLL . . .

   C = RLUUUUU . . . or RULLLLL . . .

   D = RRUUUUU . . . or RURRRRR . . .

d. The code names for any point that is at the vertex of one of the small vacant triangles must end with an infinite string of repeated letters (e.g., UURRRRRR . . . or LURULLLLL . . .).

FURTHER EXPLORATION

1. This statement is true. For any beginning sequence of a string (say URU, for example), a particular small triangle in the Sierpiński triangle is specified. Given this initial sequence, there are infinitely many strings of R's, L's, and U's (infinite in length) that could complete the sequence and describe a point in this small piece of the Sierpiński triangle. For example, say the string begins with URU; then URU UUUUU . . ., URU LLLUUULLLUUU . . . and URU RLRRLRRRL . . . are three such strings. Only those that end with . . .LLLLL . . ., . . .RRRRRR . . ., or . . .UUUUU . . . are points at the vertices of a triangle. For example, URU UUUU . . . and URLULRLU LLLLLLL . . . are two such strings. However, there are many more nonrepeating sequences than repeating sequences.

    To prove this, note that you could match every sequence that ends with LLLLLL . . . (a vertex point) to a sequence that ends with URURUR . . . (a non-vertex point); each sequence that ends UUUUU . . . to a sequence that ends RLRLRLRL . . .; and each sequence that ends RRRRRR . . . to a sequence that ends with LULULULU . . .. There would be no vertex points unaccounted for. Yet there would remain infinitely many other non-vertex points unmatched (e.g., any sequence ending with URLURLURL . . .). Therefore, there are more non-vertex points in the Sierpiński triangle than vertex points.

2. Any code name that has no U's in it will correspond to a point that lies on the base of the Sierpiński triangle.

    If you change L's to 0's and R's to 1's, then the new string of 0's and 1's corresponds to some binary number between 0 and 1. In fact, each R-L sequence corresponds to exactly one binary sequence. Now, some *pairs* of binary sequences will correspond to the same number between 0 and 1. For example, the sequences 0111 . . . and 1000 . . . both correspond to ½. Similarly, 0011111 . . . and 0100000 . . . correspond to ¼. Note that LRRRR . . . and RLLLL . . . are assigned to the same point in the Sierpiński triangle. Similarly, LLRRRR . . . and LRLLLLL . . . give the address of a single point. But the fact is that changing L's to 0's and R's to 1's yields every possible binary sequence. Similarly, for every binary number between 0 and 1, there is exactly one R-L sequence representing a point on the base of the Sierpiński triangle.

3. Reversing the letters of the code name of a target gives you all but the first two moves required to hit that target (where U corresponds to 1, 2; L corresponds to 3, 4; and R corresponds to 5, 6). Given a target in the chaos game, do any first two moves to move the point off the boundary of the original triangle and into its interior. Then select the vertices corresponding to the letters in the code name in reverse order. For example, Further Exploration problem 4(a) in Lesson 5 asks you to hit the target pictured here in the minimum number of moves. Since the location of this target is ULR, the required sequence consists of five moves of the form ___, ___, R, L, U. (In this case, since the seed is at the right vertex, choose either LU or UL as the first two moves.)

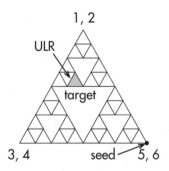